God Knows
You
Worry

God Knows You Worry

10 Ways to Put It Behind You

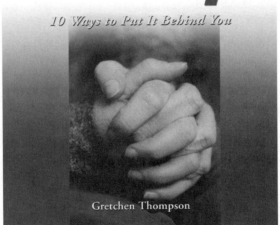

Gretchen Thompson

SORIN BOOKS   Notre Dame, Indiana

The funding exercise found in chapter nine was taken from:
Caroline Myss, Ph.D. *Why People Don't Heal and How They Can.* VHS. Mountain
Drive Productions, Faust Entertainment Corporation and Cinamedia
Corporation, 1997.

www.sorinbooks.com

International Standard Book Number: 1-893732-59-2

Cover and text design by Katherine Robinson Coleman

Printed and bound in the United States of America.

Library of Congress Cataloging-in-Publication Data
Thompson, Gretchen.
  God knows you worry : ten ways to put it behind you / Gretchen
Thompson.
    p. cm.
  ISBN 1-893732-59-2 (pbk.)
  1. Worry--Religious aspects--Christianity. 2. Peace of
mind--Religious aspects--Christianity. 3. Christian life--Unitarian
Universalist authors. I. Title.
BV4908.5 .T458 2004
248.4--dc22
                                                              2003021925

This book is dedicated to my gifted colleagues at

HealthPartners Hospice of the Lakes,

steadfast and powerful healers all.

CONTENTS

Acknowledgments

Heartfelt thanks to Travis Thompson-Ferguson for his always-gentle feedback, his willingness to help, his special expertise in the area of mind-body relationships, and his considerable research abilities.

And special gratitude to those certain teachers who inspired and blessed me with their wisdom about worry more than they will ever know: Marianne and Bill Wallace, Jim and Molly Ayers, Betty Godin, Dick Johnson and Kendra Schulte, Kent and Marlys Riedesel, Tom and Connie O'Connor, Tom and Margaret Richards, Glenn Bosacker, Phyllis Hubbard, Lois and Gene Alberg, Hulda Dolan, Johannah Puett, Betty and Doc Dockham, and last but far from least, the irrepressible Bernice Welke.

Introduction

Has your life seemed just too difficult to figure out lately?

- Have you felt overly preoccupied with national and global events?

- Do others sometimes say, "You worry too much!" or "You're too sensitive! Can't you just let it go?"

- Do things feel like they're veering out of control?

- Do you wish you could figure out how to be more carefree?

- Do you experience a heavy weight of care for others on your back?

- Does your body hold a lot of stress or tension or feel exhausted?

- Do you remember the past as a much less burdensome time?

- Has some part of your life seemed insoluble lately?

- Do you wish you were having more fun?

- Are you anxious about something in your future?

- Do you ever wonder if there's something wrong with you because you think so hard about issues that bother you?

If you answered yes to any of the above questions, I invite you to explore this book. I promise that you will learn more about worry in general and more about managing your own worries in ways that bring you peace, calm, and joy.

Worry is part of the human condition, and I doubt it will ever go away—in your lifetime, mine, or anyone else's. Some argue, in fact, that it serves an essentially positive function: Worry keeps us alert and actively engaged in those aspects of our lives that mean the very most to us.

Until it becomes too much, that is. Too pervasive. Too burdensome to our bodies, hearts, minds, and spirits.

There is such a thing as too much worry. At some point, it no longer serves that positive function of keeping us actively engaged, and instead begins to do the opposite. It can drain us, distract us, slow us down, keep us awake at night, leave us feeling wrung-out or discouraged, and actually reduce our capacity to handle the very difficulties that we seek to resolve.

When that happens, it's time to address the problem.

The good news is this: Because worry is an age-old human problem, people have grappled with it for many centuries. Wisdom abounds. Many strategies for dealing with it effectively have been tried, honed, and passed along to others. When you're caught up in worry, things can feel a bit hopeless, as though you'll never be free. Not so.

This book contains ten different ways to reduce the worry in your life. Stories, examples, exercises, and the wise words of others have all been included here to help you along your way toward a more relaxed, contented, and worry-free existence.

Though I suggest that you begin reading with chapter 1, which frames the book somewhat, feel free after that to pick any chapter that seems to fit your need or draw your attention. It is important to me that you take what you want and let go of the rest. The last thing I'd wish for you would be to worry about your worry book! I'd much prefer that you relax, enjoy, have a little fun with it, and see what you can learn.

By the way, it is no coincidence that I have authored such a book as this. Any close friend of mine will confirm that I have at times been called an expert worrier myself! I write these words as one who has truly struggled with worry and its ramifications: all the ways it can drain the soul, all the ways it can gouge into personal happiness and contentment. I approach this topic not as a distant expert, but as a humble fellow traveler.

Wishing for you that your life be increasingly free from the knit brow, the sleepless nights, the care infused with fear and anxiousness.

WAY 1 :

Learn to Locate Your Worry-Sources

TODAY IS THE TOMORROW YOU
WORRIED ABOUT YESTERDAY.

Jerry Longan

I've noticed that worry can come in different shapes and sizes. Most of us know of Little Worry and Big Worry.

Little Worry is usually time-limited and easily recognizable. Say you're tense about an upcoming annual performance review at work. A week beforehand, you start to fret about it, somewhat. The morning of the review itself, you're a bundle of nerves. By noon of that same day, however, it's over. You know what your boss has to say about you, whether positive or negative. By dinnertime, there are no more butterflies in your stomach, and you can concentrate again on other things. Little Worry has a way of resolving and then dissipating.

Big Worry is another matter. When difficulty enters your life for an extended period of time, it affects your body, mind, and spirit in complex and interrelated ways. You find yourself chronically anxious, agitated, or numb, yet sometimes unsure about the actual source of your own emotional condition. Big Worry has a way of infiltrating your life, penetrating every aspect of it like a pervasive fog.

Let's say that someone you love very much is in a car accident, and the injuries are serious. Naturally enough, you find yourself worrying about them. A month, two months, twelve months go by. Your loved one does not heal quickly, and in fact their injuries and troubles begin to impact your own life in multiple ways: financially, socially, and emotionally. You find yourself lying in bed at night unable to sleep, thoughts spinning through all these arenas. You know this is not constructive or useful, but can't seem to stop. Eventually, everything begins to feel worrisome. There are butterflies that never leave your stomach. Little things, things that used to roll off your back, no longer do.

You think you're worried about your loved one being too isolated, so you set up a phone tree that seems to work wonderfully, only to find that you're still lying awake at night, anxious about something else.

The sources of Little Worry are often obvious. The sources of Big Worry, on the other hand, are not always so obvious. And yet, it is important to locate them as best you can because this provides you with a starting point for coping with them.

Try this:

Look at the line below, marked "Continuum of Caring," and think about your own life. The far left end of this line represents the things in your life that you care about the least. Moving to the right, then, are those things increasingly important to you: things that capture your heart, engage your concern and love. The far right end of the line stands for those things that you care about most of all.

By "things" I mean people, experiences, memories, events, values, jobs, or places—whatever is part of your life and comes to mind. On the far left end of my own continuum, for example, is Zero, my son's pet lizard for whom I feel a distinct indifference. My son himself, on the other hand, belongs at the far right, along with his brother Owen and my husband Tom. My vocational field of spirituality, in which I invest a great deal of time and energy, is also toward the right end. Sending out Christmas cards is more toward the middle: I keep wishing I'd care, but to be honest, I only care enough to get it done about half the time.

Next look at the vertical line below. Let's call this your "Continuum of Power." At the top are those things in your life over which you feel you have a lot of power, mastery, or influence. Going down the line are all those things in regard to which you experience your power or mastery as decreasing or diminishing. The very bottom represents those parts of your life about which you feel most helpless.

For me, studying and learning are near the top of this continuum because I tend to take on classes with confidence and feel powerful when it comes to succeeding academically. On the other hand, cooking belongs at the bottom. Though I try to follow the recipes and do everything right, many of my final culinary products are failures. In a kitchen I often feel helpless.

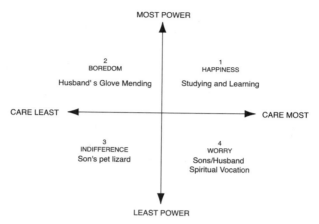

You'll notice that these two lines, intersecting in the middle, divide life into four quadrants.

Quadrant One encompasses those parts of your life where feelings of Caring and Power are both high. Often, when life carries us into this quadrant, our predominant emotion is *happiness*. This is because it's a wonderful experience to be both deeply engaged and highly effective or powerful in a given arena. For example, I am quite happy when I take a class in spiritual study. I love my field and anticipate that I'll do well while learning more about it to boot!

In Quadrant Two, the sense of Power is high, but the sense of Caring is low. The predominant emotion here is often *boredom*. My husband spent one summer in high school mending industrial gloves at a local factory—hundreds and hundreds per day, one at a time. He was quite competent and fast when it came to mending gloves; his level of Power was high. But he just didn't care about gloves at all, and consequently found the work extremely dull. It left him restless, anxious to hear that five o'clock release bell.

Quadrant Three encompasses those arenas of our lives where sense of Power and sense of Caring are both low. The most common emotion here is *indifference*. I don't have a clue about how to care for Zero, a large lizard. I know he eats several crickets and one live mouse per week, and as a lover of little creatures, I would be ineffective when it came to feeding him. Thankfully, my lack of felt power in this arena does not bother me because I don't care about Zero too much in the first place. I am basically pretty detached when it comes to my son's lizard. Lucky for him, he occupies Quadrant One in my son's life, and therefore receives excellent care in spite of my Quadrant Three indifference!

In Quadrant Four, our sense of Power is low, but our sense of Caring is high. And the most common emotion for this arena is (yes, you guessed it) *worry*. When you care deeply about something yet feel relatively helpless about it, you've entered a fertile breeding ground for all forms of worry—Little, Big, and all the sizes in between.

Take that performance review mentioned earlier. The more you value your job and want to do well *and* the more you feel helpless to influence your boss's opinion of you, the more you are apt to worry.

Worry is a natural human phenomenon, and it tends to occur in relation to those parts of our lives that occupy Quadrant Four. If you find yourself deeply worried about something or worried about you-know-not-what—just generally worried—this is not about some failure on your part. It is about being human. It is also about caring deeply, or feeling helpless, or—most likely—both.

A major first step in contending with worry is to increase your understanding about where it is coming from. Find its sources, so that you can begin to work with them.

WORRY IS THE MOST NATURAL AND
SPONTANEOUS OF ALL HUMAN FUNC-
TIONS. IT IS TIME TO ACKNOWLEDGE
THIS, PERHAPS EVEN LEARN TO DO IT
BETTER.

Lewis Thomas

Learn to Locate Your Worry-Sources

- Take some quiet time and use the blank diagram below to write down some notes about what occupies the four quadrants of your own life. This will provide you with a "map" of sorts. See if you can place all the most important dimensions of your life somewhere on this map. Focus especially on the fourth quadrant: high caring and low power. What have you placed there? What does this tell you about yourself and the things that you tend to worry about?

- You can also use this model in reverse. Identify a situation that is presently generating a lot of worry in your life, Little or Big. Now ask yourself two questions:

  - What do I care about deeply here?

  - Is there some way I feel powerless here?

- Your answers to these two questions can lead to major decisions about how to handle your worry. Maybe you need to increase your sense of power or decrease your level of engagement, as we will explore in the following chapters, but the first step is to understand where this worry is coming from.

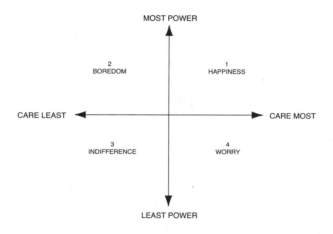

A DIFFICULTY IS AN EVENT,

THE FULL BENEFIT OF WHICH

HAS NOT YET BEEN TURNED TO YOUR

ADVANTAGE.

Anonymous

Mary Learns to Let Go

Sometimes life seems so unfair. I doubt I'll ever forget Mary, or the situation that caused her to worry herself to exhaustion.

Her little sister, Joan, after several years of yearning and hoping, finally met Stan, the man of her dreams. Mary, who had already been married for several years herself by then, was matron of honor at their wedding. Proud and happy, she stood witness to their heartfelt vows, their tender kiss, and their giggly dash to the back of the church as they set off for a honeymoon.

When Joanie and Stan had their first baby, a bald and beautiful little boy named Luke, Mary was named as his godparent. It seemed as though things were going so well. Not that Mary didn't ever worry. She did. As a loving aunt and godparent, she worried about Luke's earaches; she worried when he went to school for the first time. Sometimes she worried that Joanie, who had wanted to have more children, was having so much trouble becoming pregnant again.

But on the morning she learned that Stan had died of a heart attack at home, her worry grew in a nanosecond from Small to Big. Little Luke, six at the time, had been right there. He had seen his father's limp outstretched body, seen the terror on his mother's face, heard the scream of the ambulance sirens, and watched as strangers worked to bring life back to the lifeless form. He had been rushed to the hospital, sat in the cold waiting room for what seemed hours, and then, on top of all that, was told he would never see his father again.

Of course Mary worried about his mother as well—but she was especially concerned for Luke. Few children his age had been forced to experience such an ordeal. She gave him what she could: frequent hugs, weekends at her own home, and all kinds of assurance and tenderness. It helped to be able to do something, even if she couldn't give him back his father.

I met Mary when I entered her life as a hospice chaplain. Incomprehensible as it may seem, her sister Joanie—Luke's mother—had been diagnosed with pancreatic cancer and given only a few months to live.

Luke was nine-years-old by then, a quiet, loving boy who sometimes got teased at school for being withdrawn. His Aunt Mary immediately stepped up to the plate to take him in and raise him. She also took in his mother, so they could all be together during those final months. She took on a great deal, but of all the things that consumed her, worry about Luke's welfare was at the top of the list. How could this be happening to a little boy? And worse, how was he ever going to survive it?

Mary was doing everything she could think of—everything, and more—yet none of it was enough to quell the deep sense of dread that pervaded her life. She had Luke in the Boy Scouts and a support group at school. Two of his uncles had been recruited to take him out for fun on Saturdays. And always, when things seemed difficult for him, she continued to simply wrap him up in a big bear hug, holding him tight.

Yet the worry continued. In terms of the diagram discussed earlier, her relationship to Luke filled her fourth quadrant: she cared about him deeply, more deeply than words could tell, but at the very same time, she felt painfully powerless to help him.

Sometimes when a person finds some part of their life in the fourth quadrant, they will instinctively and even heroically try to move it to the first quadrant by exerting as much power or influence as is humanly possible. This is what Mary did. Without even being completely aware of it, she continued pouring out almost superhuman amounts of effort, trying to regain control of a situation that felt basically out of her control. Her fear was that no matter how hard she tried, she was not going to be able to change Luke's fate; that his father's death and now his mother's cancer were both more powerful than she.

Another way Mary might have escaped worry would have been to move Luke's place in her life from the fourth quadrant to the third: in other words, to care about him less. That, needless to say, was not an option for her. She loved him too much. Talk about trapped.

You can imagine how she felt when one day the principal of Luke's school called her in for a meeting. Apparently, Luke had begun acting out. How she dreaded going in there to hear about what they must all deal with next. She went anyway, of course. And was she ever shocked to hear what Luke had been up to! It could have been fighting; it could have been swearing. It could have been stealing, or skipping class, or talking back to teachers. In fact, it was hugging.

"Luke has taken to giving his teacher and the other kids hugs. Big ones, sometimes very tight ones, without asking or explaining why," the principal explained kindly. "Now we know that he is going through a lot, but he is catching people off guard, and it just needs a little management. If we could bring him in here right now, while you are here, I am sure you and I can help him figure this out."

Mary was so taken aback that she didn't know what to

say. Hugging was what she had taught Luke for those times when words were simply insufficient in the midst of pervasive sorrow. It was completely understandable that this shy, hurting boy would resort to hugs. Granted, this was not particularly appropriate in terms of social behavior at school, but it touched her deeply that he was working out his pain in such a manner.

A new thought hit her, then, almost like a lightening bolt: She had been so focused on what she had no power over—his mother's dying process, his prior losses—that she had completely overlooked what she clearly had plenty of power over. She'd had power enough to teach a little boy what to do when it hurt. Power enough to help him trust his own feelings and not hide them. Power enough to show him that the world around him could be trusted and reached out to. These were important and profoundly significant achievements on her part. Pondering them, she could almost feel strength and vitality flowing back into her mind and heart.

Mary experienced a radical internal shift. In terms of quadrants, it was actually a shift from the fourth to the first. She came to understand that she possessed both sufficient caring and sufficient power to help make this boy's life whole, despite all of its wounds. She'd been liberated at last from the crippling worry that had plagued her.

She still had to figure out about the hugs though. It wasn't that hard after all. Luke's teacher understood his need for them and so did the school counselor. Instead of waiting for him to approach them, they found him first thing each morning and wrapped their arms around him in friendly greeting, just to let him know that he was cared for and safe. They also arranged for him to go to the counselor's office any time during the day when things got rough and visit with her until he felt reassured. Luke was advised not to hug other children unless he asked first, and they consented. Actually, this rarely came up. His needs had been understood, his boundaries explained. He relaxed.

Hugs at home were identified as completely permissible. We on the hospice team were glad to help. It meant that whenever we visited, the first thing that happened would usually be a heartfelt hug from a dear little boy. We were glad to hug him back. It was a blessing for us, and an honor.

Sometimes we even hugged his Aunt Mary too.

GOD GRANT ME THE SERENITY

TO ACCEPT THE THINGS

I CANNOT CHANGE,

THE COURAGE TO

CHANGE THE THINGS I CAN,

AND THE WISDOM

TO KNOW THE DIFFERENCE.

Reinhold Niebuhr

Ned Makes It Through the Night

Sometimes you can scoot something worrisome out of Quadrant Four, but you just don't know it until you try.

My little cousin Ned was the youngest of all of us. That meant he was always somehow tagging along—a little late, a little short, or a little behind. When we played yard games, for example, he always got caught first. When we piled in the car to go for a treat at the A&W, he always got there last and consequently found himself squashed in the middle. And so on, and so forth. It was the typical life of many a last kid, no doubt. Ned was used to feeling relatively powerless in a world of people who towered over him.

We were lucky as kids because all of us cousins lived on the same block. This meant that we had, for all practical purposes, extra "siblings" to play with, multiple "mothers" to make us peanut butter sandwiches or catch us doing something wrong, and plenty of different back yards to run around in.

There were actually eight of us all together. One of our very favorite things to do was to have overnights. We'd beg our parents to say yes, grab our sleeping bags, and pile joyously into someone's attic, basement, or tree fort for a night of giggling, roughhousing, and reading comics with flashlights.

All of us except Ned, that is.

The first time Ned came along with us for an overnight, his big brother scared the living daylights out of him by pointing out monsters in every shadow. His mom had to come get him because he was crying so hard, and after that he was always too terrified to join in. Every time we even started talking about an overnight, his brows would knit into worried, fearful furrows, and he'd run home as fast as he could.

Being the second youngest myself, I felt bad for Ned. I knew he wanted a whole lot to be with us, but was just too scared of being hurt by those monsters he'd heard about to make it through the night.

I wasn't thinking of it in those terms then, but now I can see it: Ned definitely had put overnights in his fourth quadrant: high sense of caring, but low sense of power.

Ned needed to discover how brave and capable he really could be. The next time we talked about an overnight, I said, "Hey, I know, let's have it in Ned's room!"

Ned himself, for once, didn't bolt, though he did look kind of puzzled at the idea. I suppose he was wondering if the monsters would follow us all into his room. He had a chance to find out.

That night we all piled in there, up to our usual shenanigans. At midnight, stuffed with popcorn and still going strong, Ned seemed to have forgotten about the monsters altogether. By 2 a.m., sweeping his flashlight over a Superman comic, he was getting drowsy. By dawn—like all the rest of us—he was in a deep sleep.

Ned never worried about overnights again.

No need to worry about the world coming to an end today.

It's already tomorrow in Australia.

Charles Schulz

WAY 2:

Engage in Incompatible Behaviors

PEOPLE GET SO IN THE HABIT OF WORRY
THAT IF YOU SAVE THEM FROM
DROWNING
AND PUT THEM ON A BANK TO DRY IN
THE SUN WITH HOT CHOCOLATE AND
MUFFINS
THEY WONDER WHETHER THEY ARE
CATCHING COLD.

John Jay Chapman

Perhaps you remember that old game of patting your head and rubbing your stomach at the same time. It's a pretty hard combination, but most of us can learn to do it if we try hard and long enough.

Some combinations, on the other hand, are impossible to pull off no matter how much a person practices. For example, you can't walk and stand still at the same time. Neither can you simultaneously smile and frown, or shout and be silent. Sometimes, one kind of behavior simply cancels another out. When that happens, the behaviors are called incompatible.

What does that have to do with worrying?

Plenty!

It means that there are at least a few things in your own life that you simply cannot do while you are worrying, and vise versa. If you figure out what those behaviors are, and do them more, you simply worry less—no getting around it. For example, my psychologist friend Nancy has found that for several of her clients walking and worrying are incompatible behaviors. Maybe for the first part of a walk these men and women will worry as they move along, but if they keep at it—nice long walks, day after day—their worrying diminishes significantly. Their mind literally can't hold on to those old circuitous preoccupations. Strolling along in the sun and wind, arms swinging, breathing in the fresh air, they become liberated from their worries without even working at it.

Worry may return again for them later on, but simply getting a break from it serves several functions. For one thing, it helps them to remember how wonderful worry-free existence can feel. Also, it breaks up thinking patterns that may have become rigid and uncomfortable, nourishes an anxious soul, and energizes a stressed and weary body.

Referring back to the last chapter's four quadrants, think about this: It is impossible to be in two of them at the same time. You cannot feel powerful and powerless in the same moment. It is impossible to simultaneously care and not care about something. One viable way to "get out" of that worry-infested fourth quadrant then is to be intentional about devoting more time each day to one of the others.

Perhaps you have heard the story of the people from a small village in the mountains long ago whose lives had become overwhelmed with worry, anxiousness, and distrust. Fearful that their own neighbors would steal from them, they hoarded the bounty of their gardens, guarding their own harvest carefully and never sharing. Anticipating that the unkindness of others would meet them wherever they went, they stayed inside their houses, doors locked and curtains pulled tight, refusing to speak to one another. Doubting one another in all these and countless other ways, they developed strong habits of avoidance, unfriendliness, and misery. As the years passed, their village grew less and less prosperous for lack of sharing and friendliness.

At last they could tolerate it no longer. Desperately concerned for their own survival, they found their way to the hut of a wise man who lived far away in the center of a large woods.

This good man listened kindly and carefully as they described the worry and distrust that had come to cripple their hearts and threaten their well-being. And when they finished their sad tale with the question, "What should we do?" he stood silent for a long, long time.

At last he spoke. "I don't know what to tell you about your problem, but I will tell you this. One among you, believe it or not, is the Messiah, the Holy One, returned to earth to bring your own village great comfort and renewal. One among you is the holiest of all that is holy and will prove to be the source of great hope for all of you. The problem is, I do not know which one of you that is. You will have to discover that for yourselves."

As the townspeople returned home again, all kinds of new thoughts were swirling in their heads, for they had begun to look among themselves for the Messiah. Likewise, in the ensuing days as they worked in their gardens, they began to glance over toward their neighbor, wondering, "Could he be the Messiah, here to help us?" Or when someone knocked on their door, instead of tightening its lock, they would swing it open and invite the visitor in, thinking, "I must welcome this one with an open heart, for she might be the Messiah, here to help us."

Day upon day, they watched and welcomed one another in this new way, anticipating that sooner or later they would recognize the Messiah among themselves. Slowly, their distrust of one another melted. Their worry and fear were transformed into kindness and a profound new respect. Before too long, their village had returned to a state of true prosperity. For even though no single one among them had emerged as the savior, it was the looking itself, the hoping and expectation, that had saved them.

Their new-learned behavior—watching for the Messiah—was incompatible with their old behaviors— worry, distrust, and unfriendliness. By engaging in the one, they were able to liberate themselves from all the others.

How would things change for you if you were to anticipate not the problems, the difficulties, the worrisome challenges and failures in your life, but rather the experiences with holiness, blessing, and transformation? What thoughts, actions, and choices bring you feelings of hope? Of confidence, power, and well being? Whatever these are, they are likely to be incompatible with worry.

What activities remind you to smile, play more heartily, relax your clenched fists, and let go of dreaded outcomes? Whatever they are, they are likely to be incompatible with worry.

Finding incompatible behaviors may take some experimentation on your part. For example, while I love reading and am good at it, I've found through experience that it is not incompatible with worry for me. It's too easy for the stressful thoughts to creep back in between paragraphs, too easy for me to set the open book down on my chest and launch off into the most frightened and fretful corners of my mind. Fast-paced mysteries work far better than magazines or newspaper articles, but even they aren't failsafe.

Cooking for a crowd comes much closer. Church volunteering—especially alongside others—is even better. Yoga, exercise, laughter, daydreaming or planning, sometimes work, sometimes creative endeavor, or travel, or exploration of new arenas: the list of behaviors potentially incompatible with worry is endless.

DWELLING ON THE NEGATIVE SIMPLY CONTRIBUTES TO ITS POWER.

Shirley MacLaine

Engage in Incompatible Behaviors

- Write down all the things you did yesterday—activities, projects, scheduled events, or commitments. Circle those activities that were particularly stressful or worrisome, and underline those that were incompatible with stress. How did things balance out? How might you be more intentional about scheduling in incompatible behaviors today?

- Make an agreement with yourself to try something you've never done before. Whether it is once a week or once a month, commit to keep with the schedule you've established. Learn Pinochle, go kayaking, volunteer at a non-profit organization—it doesn't matter what it is! Chances are that if you are learning how to do something new, even if you find out that you don't like it, your mind will not stray to worrisome thoughts.

• As mentioned before, go for a walk. But if you want to experiment with another incompatible behavior almost as foolproof, try laughter. Just as it is impossible to frown while you are smiling, it is difficult to laugh and worry at the same time. Do something each day that ensures a bit of joy, a touch of laughter, even if it's as simple as reading the comics. For that matter, making others laugh is as therapeutic as laughing yourself. Pay attention to joy and its healing powers.

WORRY DOES NOT EMPTY TOMORROW OF SORROW——IT EMPTIES TODAY OF STRENGTH.

Corrie ten Boom

But What About the Gifts?

Back in my community organizing days, I spent a lot of time and energy trying to improve neighborhoods. When you work in that arena for a while, you begin to notice how prevalent crime and poverty are in certain pockets of the city, and how absent they are in others.

And if you take it a step further, you can even get data and statistics about those bad neighborhoods: that there were this-many homicides in the last month, that-many robberies, this-many households unemployed, that-many children on the free lunch program at school.

Back in those days, we used the statistics to create our game plan. If poverty was the big problem, we'd see if we could leverage jobs for people. If crime was high, we'd try to get the police department to pay more attention.

The work was important. I never doubted that, but it was also discouraging some days. It was an uphill battle for those of us trying to organize change, but especially for those who lived in those neighborhoods, good and caring people who deserved better.

One day, Nadine Sims changed everything. Nadine had lived in this particular neighborhood a long time. She'd seen it in its heyday. She'd seen it deteriorate, what with the housing stock decline, the rough stuff after dark, the whole bit. She knew most of the people. And she was elderly and smart. She brought this idea to our monthly community meeting one summer day, and it caught on like wildfire.

Actually I think Nadine learned about it in the library. She'd read about another neighborhood that decided to make change happen in a completely different way than what you'd expect. Instead of inventorying their problems, their failures, and their liabilities, they decided to inventory their gifts. Instead of letting problems dictate what to do next, they decided to let successes take the lead.

It's a radical idea. But the truth of it is, you can't focus on sad things and happy things at the same time. You can't base change on failure and success at the same time. It had never occurred to us to simply change our focus.

Here's how we proceeded, with Nadine at the helm. The first thing we did was set aside all the studies that proved we had a lot of problems. Heck, we already knew that! Who needed the details? We just set those reports aside, let them gather dust in a corner somewhere.

Next we formed little interview teams and trained them to go to every home in the neighborhood. Their job was to fill out a gifts inventory on every single person: a list of things that person could do or teach that might help out others.

As you can guess, the interviews alone had a great effect on the neighborhood. It's not encouraging to talk about all your problems, but it's downright fun to share your gifts! People were eager to talk, had fun together, got to know each other in a whole different way.

The third step was to compile our data. That was by far the most amazing part. We learned, for example, that even though our grade school had lost its music teacher because of funding cuts, there were more than thirty adults within a five-block radius of the school who could sing or play an instrument. We called them up and asked them if they would volunteer. More than half said yes right away. All of a sudden our kids had a whole new music program.

There were hardly any restaurants in our neighborhood because businesses were afraid to come there. In our inventory we learned that there were three ladies just blocks away from one another that were fantastic cooks. Within a year, the three of them had gotten together, applied for a loan from a bank, and opened up a little soul food restaurant next to the grocery store. I don't need to tell you how happily the rest of the neighborhood supported that operation.

If you're paying attention to bad stuff, it's easy to forget good stuff. We were blessed to learn that the opposite is also true. We paid attention to the good stuff, and let the bad take a rest. It worked. I can't quote any crime statistics for that neighborhood, but I can tell you where to go if you want to learn how to play the horn, who can fix your plumbing or your roof, and where to buy a big, nourishing plate of soul food.

The power of Nadine's vision was something I hope I never forget.

John Michaels

BIRDS SING AFTER A STORM; WHY SHOULDN'T PEOPLE FEEL AS FREE TO DELIGHT IN WHATEVER SUNLIGHT REMAINS TO THEM?

Rose Kennedy

Tossing Worry Out the Window

Jim and Robert occupied the same room in a nursing home. Both men were suffering from chronic health conditions that left them bed-bound most of the time. Jim's bed, however, was right next to the room's only window, while Robert's faced an inside wall.

Robert and Jim got to know one another quite well over time. They told one another all about their lives: their families, homes, jobs, military service, hobbies, and favorite vacations. They also spent hours talking about the worries they faced: their fears about failing their families, their concerns about certain children, or the uncertainty of the future.

Every afternoon, Jim would spend a brief time sitting up, and pass the time by telling Robert about all that he could see as he looked out the window. Robert, for his part, came to appreciate this greatly, for the only scenario within his own reach was a dull landscape of painted walls, metal equipment, and glaring overhead lights. It was a great delight for him to hear about what lay beyond that window: the beautiful deep green lawn of a city park, the sparkling pond where fountains arched and swans floated gracefully and where children splashed and played. He loved to hear Jim tell about the lovers strolling arm in arm, the lush gardens of roses, tulips, and daffodils, the beloved and familiar city skyline that arched grandly behind it all.

As Jim spoke, Robert would close his eyes and imagine each scene in exquisite detail. For a brief time then, he would be transported from his own world of worry and pain into places of much greater beauty, bounty, and joy.

So passed weeks and then months, with Jim offering Robert description upon description of life outside the nursing home: passing parades, rainstorms, friendly baseball games, lavish picnics, romping dogs, and mother ducks leading their ducklings into the water.

There came a morning that the nurse entered their room as usual, only to discover that Jim had died peacefully in his sleep during the night. This was a difficult loss for Robert, and he lay in bed grieving for days. At last, though, he asked the nurse if he might be moved over to Jim's unoccupied bed. It occurred to him that the least he could do in honor of his old friend would be to take up that same post by the window and witness the wonderful view that Jim had so kindly described for him all along.

The nurse was glad to look into his request, and before the day was over, Robert found himself in Jim's old bed. At first he simply lay there, adjusting to the change. But after a few hours, he knew he was ready. He managed to prop himself up on a weak elbow, and then strained to take a first look out the window that Jim had spoken about so often.

Imagine Robert's surprise when he gazed out and saw that the view from Jim's window was nothing but the large, looming, ugly wall of an adjacent building.

Jim had understood all along that the beauty of the outside world would be incompatible with his roommate's worries. He'd also understood that the view itself required not excellent scenery as much as excellent imagination.

What a monumental gift he had given his friend.

Sometimes, incompatible behaviors can involve dreams, wishes, or imaginary images. This makes them no less liberating and no less real.

In honor of Jim, close your eyes and conjure up a scene for your own life that leaves worry far behind. Dwell there; rest there for as long as you would like to.

Don't worry, the real world with all its real problems will intrude soon enough. You have nothing to lose and much to gain by taking a little break.

LIKE WATER WHICH CAN CLEARLY
MIRROR THE SKY AND THE TREES
ONLY SO LONG AS ITS SURFACE IS
UNDISTURBED,
THE MIND CAN ONLY REFLECT THE TRUE
IMAGE OF THE SELF
WHEN IT IS TRANQUIL AND WHOLLY
RELAXED.

Indra Devi

WAY 3 :

Interrupt Yourself—Gently

WELL IF YOU WANT TO SING OUT,
SING OUT;
AND IF YOU WANT TO BE FREE, BE FREE.
THERE ARE A MILLION WAYS TO BE,
YOU KNOW THAT THERE ARE.

Maude, in Harold and Maude

I've always liked the following little teaching tale:

A woman going out for a walk on a sunny day falls unexpectedly into a gigantic hole right in the middle of the street. Shocked and confused, bruised and sore, she sits in the damp darkness of this hole for quite a while before gathering herself together, climbing out, and continuing on her way.

The next time she goes for a walk, she heads down the same street, and having forgotten all about the hole steps right into it a second time, tumbling once more into its clammy depths. Again, she just sits there for a while in disbelief, shakes herself off, regains her bearings, and then climbs out.

The third time she goes for a walk, even as she's thinking to herself, "Surely, they've repaired that hole by now!" she accidentally steps into the same darned hole and tumbles down into the darkness. This time, however, she's feeling pretty frustrated and sits down there for just a short while before climbing out, eager to be done with this cursed situation.

The fourth time she sets out for a walk, she just knows they've repaired the hole by now, and is shocked beyond belief when she falls into it again. This time, even on her way down, she whispers to herself, "When will I ever learn?" and jumps right out again, as quickly as she can.

The fifth time she goes out for a walk, determined to avoid the same old tumble, she chooses a different path down the street.

The sixth time she goes out for a walk, she finally chooses a different street.

In a way, worry can be like a big, deep, dark hole right in the middle of the street that is your daily life. You may know perfectly well that it's there and have every intention of avoiding it, but even so, you're used to walking down that particular street. It's a habit, and habits are hard to break. You sometimes find yourself tumbling down into a state of worry even when you don't mean to.

It takes time to change. Learning new paths and breaking old habits takes practice. This is why interrupting your worry, while it really can help you "re-route" yourself, so to speak, needs to be done very gently and in a spirit of true self-respect. After all, falling into the hole itself is painful enough without heaping self-criticism in there on top of it. Learn to interrupt your old worry-patterns gently, and before you know it, you too may be walking down a whole new street, headed in a whole new direction.

The quotation that begins this chapter is taken from one of the best and funniest movies about interrupting worry that I have ever seen, *Harold and Maude.* Harold, a young man whose life is quite difficult and fraught with all kinds of worries, has simply lost his ability to "climb out of the hole." Deeply convinced that he is destined to suffer without escape, he buys a secondhand hearse and starts to randomly attend the funerals of strangers because it is only in such contexts that he can feel at home.

Enter Maude: full of life and love, four times his age, and several times wiser than he in the ways of joy and suffering. Seeing that Harold can only focus on what he is worried about, she does not scold him or tell him to knock it off. She gently interrupts him, tenderly invites him to dance, or sings him a little song, or simply hands him a piece of her amazingly delicious ginger pie.

Because his patterns of worry are so deeply ingrained, he at first can barely notice her, much less understand what she is trying to offer him. But like any good teacher, she continues to interrupt his worry again and again, in all kinds of ways. Maude shows Harold some of her wildly creative and odd inventions, invites him to learn a tune on her old banjo, and takes him for a drive to a huge field of flowers and for a ride on a motorcycle. Very gradually, under her tutelage, he learns to not only climb out of the old hole, but eventually to avoid it altogether, and finally, to sing his way down a whole new street.

When Maude dies at the end of the movie—a heartbreaking loss for Harold—he has learned so much from her about interrupting worry and sorrow that he knows now how to handle even this most difficult turn of events. And in the final scene, we see him setting off with his banjo, playing the tune she'd sung for him long ago: "If you want to sing out, sing out; and if you want to be free, be free. There are a million ways to be."

Believe me, if Harold can learn to interrupt his worry—gently and with self-respect—so can we. It involves a bit of talking back to yourself, perhaps a bit of imagination, but you may find that it's easier than you think. The following exercises should help.

I WORRY ABOUT THE FUTURE AND I WORRY ABOUT THE PAST.

I WORRY THAT MY SAVINGS AND MY IRA WON'T LAST.

I WORRY ABOUT POLITICS AND WORLD AFFAIRS AND SUCH,

BUT MOST OF ALL I WORRY THAT I WORRY MUCH TOO MUCH.

Thomas Swallen

Interrupt Yourself–Gently

- Imagine setting up a "worry firewall" in your mind. Firewalls, as you may know, are those walls in a building specifically designed to prevent fire from passing through. The term can also refer to certain security measures in a computer system that block out unwanted data or information. Pick some specific worries you'd like to be free of and imagine setting up a firewall against them inside your mind. Just the idea of being able to block them out is more powerful than you might expect and will possibly interrupt them quite effectively right away. In my experience, however, certain worries still try to sneak past my imaginary firewall, and I have to be on my toes, notice, and remind myself to keep the wall intact and in force.

- Sometimes, just whispering the word "firewall" can send unwanted worries scurrying, but I have been known to shout out "Firewall!" in public places, just to keep certain peskier ones at bay. This is guaranteed to start an interesting conversation.

- Along those same lines, Eugene Walker, in his fine book *Learn to Relax*, talks about "thought-stopping." In his own words: "Get the thought that has been a problem firmly in mind. You then shout very loudly, 'Stop! Stop! Stop!' You may pound your fist on the table for emphasis. This is repeated several times. Next, practice saying it mentally while thinking about pounding your fist." According to Walker, you can quickly extinguish worries or anxieties in this demonstrative manner. Notice that he encourages you to direct a kind of firmness or anger not at yourself, but at the worrisome thought you wish to influence.

- Close your eyes. Focus on something you are worried about and come up with a symbol for it—a shorthand image that represents it. Now imagine putting it in a box. Even if the image—the worry—is huge, imagine that the box is even bigger—big enough to contain it. Now imagine the box shrinking, shrinking, shrinking down until it is much smaller. Imagine it turning into a bird. Imagine the bird flying away, away, and away, until it becomes nothing more than a pinpoint on the horizon, and disappears. Repeat as often as needed.

- If you're due for a chuckle anyway (see previous chapter) go to the movie store and rent *Harold and Maude*. Actually, any comedy would probably serve as appropriate interruption!

- Pick up the book *Feeling Good*, by Dr. David Burns, a masterpiece in the art of interrupting worries and all kinds of other negative thoughts. This is an excellent book, and a compelling read.

Worry is a habit acquired through repetition.

I am learning that I can change my worry and negative thoughts through conscious, deliberate practice.

I can cultivate good habits through repetition, just as I once cultivated bad ones.

Anonymous, from a Twelve Step Program

Almost There

When I was a kid, we would go to my grandmother's house in Minneapolis every Christmas, starting from Chicago and driving straight through. This was hardly an easy trip. There weren't freeways back then, so the journey involved getting jiggled awake early in the morning when it was still dark, piling into our old station wagon that was already packed to bursting with gifts, clothes, food, and the dog, and heading off down the highway, knowing I'd be crammed uncomfortably between my two brothers for at least twelve hours.

I remember, especially in my younger years, feeling like this trip was going to take forever. Filled with pre-Christmas anticipation already, I couldn't imagine how I was going to endure such a long period of enforced stillness. I was the one in the family famous for asking that question that drove my father close to insane: Are we almost there yet?

He was always the driver, and he was always going as fast as he dared. If I think about it now, I realize that the trip was probably harder on him than anyone else in the family. He didn't have a whole lot of patience with my question, but he tried.

I tried too. First, I'd think of every gift I hoped to get, and then every gift I was going to give, all of them wrapped up now in bright paper and packed behind me. Then I'd pat the dog. Then I'd sing all the Christmas carols I could remember under my breath. And then, when I absolutely couldn't stand it a minute longer, I'd say, "Daddy, are we almost there?"

He'd answer in a measured way through clenched teeth, "Not yet, dear. We're about one hour out, with eleven to go. Try not to ask again until we at least reach Milwaukee."

I'd watch the phone wires loop, loop, looping past me from pole to pole out the window until I felt woozy in the stomach. I'd nibble on soda crackers that my mother brought. Then I'd breathe on the back window to make a frosty fog and draw pictures in it. Poke my brother. Wiggle my toes. Try to take a nap.

"Daddy, *now* are we almost there?"

One time, when I had asked that dread question for what must have been the umpteenth time, my father—who smoked back then but has blessedly quit since—answered me kindly enough, "No, not yet, Dear." Simultaneously, however, he flicked his glowing cigarette butt out the slightly open front window with an intensity that betrayed how he was actually feeling. Unbeknownst to all of us, the thing happened to fly back in the rear window, which my brother had cracked open himself for a little fresh air.

A few minutes down the road, my other brother piped up, "Hey, the duffel bag in back here is on fire!" Sure enough, we all turned around to see smoke pouring out of it and the glowing edges of burning canvas. It was scary.

My father lurched over to the edge of the road and shouted for my mother to take the dog and us into the winter fallow field at the side of the road. She led us far from the danger in silent single file, and then we turned to watch.

It was dark out, and the moon's milky light poured down onto the snow-covered field in a dream-like way. Stars were everywhere. We watched wide-eyed as my father yanked boxes and suitcases from the rear of the station wagon, at one point taking off his jacket and beating out a burst of flame with it. I remember being filled with fear that somehow he might catch on fire and be killed. I wondered if the car might explode.

After a while—not too long, after all—he called us back. My mother helped him reload the car, then my brothers and the dog and I were told to climb back in.

Nothing had been so seriously damaged that the grown ups were too angry or worried. I think, in fact, that mostly they were relieved. After all, our family remained essentially safe and intact. That was a gift greater than any of the ones packed away behind us, some singed or smoke damaged.

I still remember to this day how, for me, everything had somehow changed. My incessant worrying, watching, and waiting—my insistent need to ask, "Are we almost there?"—had completely disappeared. Something about the fire had profoundly interrupted my preoccupations, and left me in a different frame of mind. I rode the rest of the way in dreamy, contented silence. I thought about how much I loved my mother and father, how much I loved Christmas, and how good it felt to be warm and safe, snuggled in the back seat between my two brothers.

That was the night I learned that "Almost There" can actually be a place unto itself—Somewhere—a place where worry need not dominate, and there remains plenty of room for peace of mind, and love.

Janice Olafson

TODAY I WILL CHOOSE TO BE AT PEACE
INSTEAD OF TORMENTING MYSELF WITH
USELESS WORRY.

from Today a Better Way

Fear, Faith, and Leading the Flock

According to research data, the act of speaking in public typically generates more fear than just about any other human endeavor. In fact, it comes in second only to death itself as a source of dread or anxiousness for most folks. In other words, public speaking causes a lot of worry!

As a young seminarian and then a pastor, I loved the art and practice of ministry. I loved to lend a compassionate listening ear, loved leading small groups in Biblical study or theological exploration, loved the times of rejuvenating meditation and prayer.

It was the preaching that got me. Sunday after Sunday, getting up in front of all those people—people who had come there especially to hear words of hope and healing—terrified me every time.

Around Tuesday morning, the worry would begin. What was I going to talk about in just five days? Would it be of any use to anyone? Would I be able to find the right issues to delve into? The right words? Would I embarrass myself, this time, with a real flop of a sermon? Would they all fall asleep on me or whisper to one another about how poor the message had been that day?

By Wednesday, I had to produce a sermon title for the church bulletin. That made me feel trapped, and my worry level invariably went up a few notches.

On Friday, I'd often spend the whole day working at a word processor, trying to write something worthwhile.

Saturday night, then, would almost always find me frantically revising, moving around ideas, quotes, and stories until the wee hours, desperate with fear, dread, and anxiety.

Sunday morning, bleary-eyed, I'd sit up there in the pulpit chair with a huge knot in my stomach. And basically, the knot stayed there until the sermon had been preached, the closing prayer spoken, and the church emptied of parishioners.

Sunday afternoons—and often most of Mondays— were glorious, wonderful, worry-free stretches. Stretches that I desperately needed to rebound from the stress.

But they weren't long enough.

Come Tuesday, the cycle would begin again.

It didn't show. I know it didn't. You could've asked any one of my flock if the shepherd quaked in his sandals Sunday mornings, and they would have denied it. Furthermore, folks in general were quite pleased and inspired by my sermons. I appeared to be a gifted, confident, and perhaps even bold speaker.

But it wasn't so. I was sick with worry a lot of the time.

This is a hard thing to sustain. Also, it's the opposite of faithful—contrary to what you might expect from someone in my particular profession. Why could I not have faith that, by God's grace, I would be made "good enough" up there in that pulpit? Why could I not trust in my heart that, even where I might fail as a person, God would inspire and uphold me? I was up there preaching about stuff I couldn't even seem to practice: faith, trust, hope, and grace. In my own eyes, I was a hypocrite.

Late one Saturday night—or more likely it was very early on a Sunday morning—I was wrangling with the text of my sermon as usual—hating it, fearing it, but most of all dreading the thought of speaking it in public—when I had a brand new thought.

In retrospect, I actually believe that this thought was not of my own creation, but rather sent to me by an angel, perhaps, or a messenger from God. In any case, it interrupted my worrying like no other thought had ever before managed to do.

The thought was simply this: You've done your best, and that's all that you can do. Let go now, and leave the rest to God. When I really let this thought into my mind and heart and soul I knew that it was true. I really had done my best. Really had brought my best intentions to bear upon the task, and applied my best wisdom, my best gifts of language. And now it was time to let go. I printed the thing out, set it on the table, and fell immediately into a deeply restful—if rather short—sleep.

Sunday by church time, the old familiar knot had come back again and was wreaking its havoc right in the pit of my stomach. For a moment I surrendered to it, but then I turned once again to the thought: Had I done my best? Yes, I had. Time to take a deep breath, and leave the rest to God. This immediately interrupted my anxiety and allowed me to relax into a state of trust and faith.

I know this may sound too simple, but it has served me ever since. Quite often, worry and anxiety about preaching still rise up in me. Sometimes, they even have me sliding frantically down a slippery slope by Saturday night. But if I can call up the thought that I've really, truly done my best and the rest is up to God, I find solid ground again.

It is true, don't you think?

We are only human.

We can only do so much.

The rest is out of our hands, and worrying doesn't put it back into them.

Pastor James R. Olson

MY LORD GOD, OFTEN I HAVE NO IDEA WHERE I AM GOING, AND DO NOT SEE THE ROAD AHEAD. . . . BUT I KNOW THAT I DESIRE TO PLEASE YOU, AND THAT IF I DO NOT DEPART FROM THAT DESIRE, YOU WILL LEAD ME BY THE RIGHT ROAD, EVEN THOUGH I KNOW NOTHING ABOUT IT. THEREFORE I WILL TRUST YOU ALWAYS, EVEN WHEN I FEEL LOST AND IN THE SHADOW OF DEATH. AND I WILL NOT FEAR, FOR YOU ARE EVER WITH ME.

Adapted from Thomas Merton

WAY 4:

Help Your Body Help Your Mind

WE ALL KNOW THAT WORRY RESIDES IN
THE BODY. IT HAS TO.
IF WE HAD NO BODY, WE WOULD HAVE
NO WORRY——OR ANYTHING ELSE.
WORRY MUST BE, AT LEAST IN PART, A
PHYSICAL CONDITION.

Edward Hallowell

The other day I met my cousin Janet for lunch. A long time had passed since we'd gotten together. While working full-time at a high powered job, she'd been consumed for several months now by caring for her beloved little dog, Fannie, who had cancer. I noticed almost immediately that she had lost a lot of weight. Since this was a goal both of us had somewhat jokingly aspired to for several years now, I congratulated her. She just looked at me.

"I haven't been trying at all," she explained, her eyes tired and her shoulders sagging. "This is what's known as the Worry Diet."

Worry is sometimes connected to weight loss, and other times to weight gain. It can cause too much sleep or too little. It can produce ulcers, stiffness, clamminess, jitters, sluggishness, aches, fever, and feelings of suffocation—all sorts of physical symptoms. Even though we usually think of worry as something that happens in the mind, it is deeply connected to the functions of the body.

This truth has both good news and bad news embedded in it. The bad news: Worry has the power to cause all kinds of bodily suffering. The good news: Interventions via the body can do a great deal to diminish or even obliterate worry. This chapter focuses on the good news.

Yes, you may be quite concerned about being frustratingly overweight, about smoking cigarettes to calm your nerves, about drinking too much, or lying awake all night, about the terrible tightness in your neck from stress, or some other physical symptom of accumulated worry in your life. Sometimes it may seem that unless you get some of these things under control, your anxiety will just continue to circle round, compounding itself—mind to body to mind to body and back to mind again—until you break down completely.

We can break the cycle. In fact, here are three things that help your body to help your mind when it comes to worry. Engage any one of these or any combination of them, and your worry will begin to diminish. These three ways are like bright threads running through the complex tapestry of your worry. Start pulling on any one of them, and the whole thing begins to unravel. Simple as that.

The first of these—possibly the most important—is to move. If you sit still, worry will hunker down in your body and grip your bones. It is immobilizing mentally, and it can also be immobilizing physically. Therefore, simply moving—re-mobilizing your body—can make a huge difference.

I'm not talking about setting up overblown expectations for yourself. No need whatsoever to become an Olympic skater, a pro baseball player, or a Rockette. No need, in fact, to even promise yourself that you'll walk three miles a day come hell or high water or make it to the gym every single night after work. Such expectations are often set-ups for self-criticism, which only intensifies your worry later on.

I'm talking about smaller goals: a walk around the block when you're fretting about something at work or taking a moment to swing your arms in big wide circles a few times and stretching toward the sky. Some folks say that the gentle rhythmic movement of rocking in a rocking chair can alleviate worry. Dancing for a bit to a tune on the radio or rolling your head around on your neck until the muscles loosen up both might do the trick.

Really, movement dissipates worry. Many times when the mind becomes highly anxious, the body often goes into a kind of primal "fight or flight" state. It tightens, braces itself for anything, and on a deep cellular level prepares you to move with great intensity. Your body wants to make sure you can "move through" whatever has you tense or worried. To hold it still at such times is truly counterproductive.

Now, we all know that some people really do work out at the gym every night, or run several miles each day, or swim several laps in the pool. But if you ask them how they got into such patterns, they will often tell you a story about some major worry or problem that they gradually overcame through movement. Then the activity became so healing that they just kept going. Usually it's a process, and the process begins with smaller movements and works its way into greater, steadier ones.

The second physical way to reduce worry is to breathe. Jon Kabat-Zinn, leader of the well-known Stress Reduction Clinic at the Massachusetts Medical Center, teaches his clients first and foremost to take deep, cleansing breaths as an antidote to stress or worry. Under his tutelage, they learn to discern how their breath patterns change when they are anxious or worried and how they can use intentional breath patterns to bring themselves back to a state of calm. Kabat-Zinn also teaches clients yoga, meditation, and several other techniques. However, in his own words, "When we surveyed several hundred patients who had been out of the program for a number of years and asked them what the single most important thing they got out of the program was, the majority said, 'The breathing.'"

Healthy breathing is simple: Breathe in as fully as your lungs will let you, allowing the air to flow way down toward your stomach. Now breathe out just as deeply. Now breathe in calm, and breathe out tension. Breathe in healing, breathe out hurt. Breathe in joy, breathe out sorrow. Breathe in well-being, breathe out worry.

Again, this is a very simple act, but a person can also make quite a study of it. Almost invariably, it helps a great deal.

The third way to help reduce fear and anxiousness through bodily means is to nourish yourself well. Certain foods, certain eating patterns, will help you with worry, and others will make it worse. It's common knowledge that too much coffee, chocolate, sugary desserts, or fast foods can "wire" us, making our body jittery, and consequently making worry harder to cope with. Frustratingly, these are often the foods we turn to for comfort when we're worried in the first place.

Overeating, undereating (like my cousin Janet), or disorders like anorexia and bulimia can also emerge during times of increased worry. In fact, of the three ways named here, self-nourishment may be the trickiest, because eating in our culture already plays a complex and often distinctly unhelpful role in relation to worry.

It's okay to start slow. If you typically skip breakfast and then binge at bedtime, eating your way through a day's worth of high anxiety, try adding peanut butter on toast in the morning. See what happens. If you crave high-sugar, low-nutrient comfort foods like puddings and pies when you're worried, slow down and stand back for just a moment. Ask yourself where the craving is really coming from. Will pudding really help?

Experiment. Try visiting a juice bar one day. Ask the barista what he or she would recommend for a rookie juice-drinker. See how your body reacts to a good dose of juiced carrots, celery, and lemons. Or, at a fast-food place order one of those salads in addition to, or instead of, your burger!

These three simple physical acts—eating well, breathing deeply, and moving—are profoundly interrelated. Becoming intentional about one will likely lead you, in time, to greater intentionality about the others. But it really is a process, and sometimes a slow one. Pick out what you can handle, and celebrate every success. Know that—no matter the pace—you have undertaken the wonderful task of helping your body to help your mind.

Your worrying can only decrease.

OVER THE YEARS OUR BODIES BECOME
WALKING AUTOBIOGRAPHIES,
TELLING STRANGERS AND FRIENDS ALIKE
OF THE MINOR AND MAJOR STRESSES OF
OUR LIVES.

Marilyn Ferguson

Help Your Body Help Your Mind

- Begin with what sounds easiest or most likely to help. If you have a history of struggling with eating habits, for example, start instead by improving your breathing or moving. Both of these eventually impact eating anyway. Or if you smoke a lot and even one deep breath hurts, begin by adding gentle exercise, stretching, or improved eating patterns.

- Find others to be with as you exercise and improve how you care for your body-self. Somehow, this helps most of us keep going with new practices we wouldn't otherwise be able to maintain. Walking along with friends, chatting about this or that over a chef salad, breathing all together in a yoga class, you can even forget what you are doing. By the time you're done, your worries—through little felt effort on your part— can be significantly reduced. And your body will feel great!

- If you want to replace worry with walking, here is a simple plan for starting a regular regimen of walking: Week one, stroll at a comfortable pace for about ten minutes each day. The next week, increase the amount of time that you walk by one minute each day; work up to a brisk walk. During the next few weeks, try to aim at walking forty minutes each day at an energetic pace. Most important, enjoy the walk: think constructive thoughts, consider all the gifts you have been given, attend to the life around you.

- Once every day, try to eat something slowly and deliberately, focusing all of your attention on just eating. I recommend fruit or raw vegetables. For example, if you are eating an orange, peel it slowly, smell the fragrance, feel the spray of the juice. Eat each slice one by one, rolling the slice in your mouth, consciously biting down, chewing slowly. In short, make eating one thing into a meditation every day. This way food becomes an act of thankfulness, awareness, and pleasure. Besides, one common piece of advice for those reforming their eating is to do it more slowly.

- Try to find short periods, even three or four minutes, every day to just breathe. You will be amazed at how refreshing these little breaks can be to body and spirit. Find a comfortable position: many people feel that they can breathe most readily sitting in a straight-backed chair. Then focus your attention on your own breathing. Breathe deeply and slowly so that your inflated lungs push out your abdomen. You can check this by putting your hands on your lower abdomen; feel your breath pushing your hands outward. Listen to your breath coming in slowly and steadily; listen to your breath flowing out. Your in-breaths and out-breaths should take about the same length of time. Focusing on your breathing can calm your mind. If a lot of thoughts distract you, just let them go and return to listening to your breath. At the end of your "breath-catching" time, stand up, stretch, smile, and continue with your daily activities.

- Keep it simple. Worry thrives on complexity and drama, on circuitous thinking and lack of motion. It hardly knows how to handle one great big cleansing breath, one fresh, crisp apple, or one cheerful, brisk climb up the stairs. Give your own body such gifts as these, and in time your immunity to worry will increase greatly. Resolve to move each day in some manner that stretches your body and opens your mind and heart. And if you feel hesitant, remember, "You can't steal second base and keep one foot on first."

THE BODY HAS ITS OWN WAY OF KNOWING,

A KNOWING THAT HAS LITTLE TO DO WITH LOGIC, AND MUCH TO DO WITH TRUTH.

Marilyn Sewell

Worry, Work, and Walking

I lost my management position in a major local business when our kids were four and two years old. It wasn't so much about poor performance on my part. The company was downsizing, and a large percentage of employees were released.

The company provided us with some severance pay, and also some placement services. However, the job market was depressed, and there simply weren't many positions to be found—especially at management level.

We were younger back then, my wife and I, and shorter on foresight than we should have been. We'd invested in a beautiful little home in a nice neighborhood. We had two cars—one older and paid for, the other brand new and requiring monthly payments. We didn't think about money much, and our savings account was pretty thin. My wife was staying home with the kids.

Job loss under those circumstances was a tremendous shock. At first, I was determined to solve the problem, and solve it fast. I took on my job search as though it were a job in itself: up each morning early, dressed in a suit and tie, and out the door to network, interview, explore, research— and find something new. But the longer things didn't work out, the harder that kind of attitude became to sustain.

Eventually, the placement coach I'd been working with framed two likely scenarios for me: either I'd have to move my family to a new part of the country or I'd have to re-train for a different kind of position. He estimated that the process, in either case, might take up to two years. He encouraged me to pick one scenario and run with it.

That's when I became just about immobilized with worry: worry about losing the house, about the kids and their needs, about our future, about what I should do. My wife had gone back to work part-time as a substitute teacher and that brought in some money, but not nearly enough to cover our costs. We were quickly moving toward disaster. I remember sitting on the couch in the living room, watching the kids while my wife was at work and feeling like I'd never find a solution. None of the ideas I came up with seemed right, but they all kept running around and around in my head almost like rats trapped in a maze.

My job coach was a smart guy. He could see what was happening, and encouraged me to try some new strategies for self-maintenance under stress. I don't remember a lot of what he said, but I do remember the one idea that worked for me, even though I doubted it greatly at first.

He told me to take a walk each day. "It may seem like a waste of time," he said, "but you'll be surprised how even twenty minutes of walking can slough off the strain and allow new ideas to emerge."

At first I thought he was pretty far off base, but it turns out he was absolutely right. If I got up early enough when the rest of the family was still sleeping, I could get in a good, long walk first thing. I felt its effects almost immediately. For one thing, it allowed me to begin each day with fresh air and a chance to look up at the sky. That alone lifted my spirits. But even better, it somehow settled my body down to handle the day's stresses. Arms swinging, legs stretching, I could almost feel the worries flowing out of my psyche. And eventually, flowing in to replace them, were fresh new ideas about how to proceed, what to try.

Those walks also helped me sleep better at night, and kept my appetite in balance. They quickly became the most productive, generative part of my day. In fact, even now— a year later—I'm still taking them.

Before work, that is!

John Casey

MY GRANDMOTHER STARTED WALKING FIVE MILES A DAY WHEN SHE WAS SIXTY—

SHE'S NINETY-SEVEN TODAY AND WE DON'T KNOW WHERE IN THE HELL SHE IS.

Ellen DeGeneres

Turning Points

I find this truly strange, but nobody believes me when I tell them what I've been through. My childhood was a pretty scary thing. I spent a lot of it hiding from a really mean father and feeling deserted by a mother too weak to protect me. By the time I was sixteen, I was desperate for some kind of control over my life and had become a full-blown anorexic, not that anybody in my family noticed. I finally figured out how to get over anorexia: the great answer, for me? Bulimia!

I moved out of the house as fast as I could get out, living on my own at eighteen. Bulimia is hardly fun. It's hard on your body, your self-esteem—hard on everything. I hated myself pretty thoroughly by then and was tremendously relieved when I figured out how to get over that: the great answer, for me? Drinking alcohol! And just for good measure, I threw in cigarettes.

My life wasn't exactly successful, but I was trying my hardest, and at least getting by. I worried about losing my job, I worried about my family—especially the little sister I'd left behind, and I worried about what was going to happen to me. But most of the time, I worried about nothing in particular because I was too drunk.

In treatment before the age of thirty, I tried my best (again). And failed. Well, I lasted for three months, actually, and then failed.

After sloshing around for a few more years, I landed in treatment one more round, and this time, for some reason, it took. That is a no-good, no-win feeling, let me tell you. Having to face all your junk, all your horrible memories of the past, all your terrible fears about the future, and all your shames and regrets without a single drop of booze to ease the pain. It's like your worst nightmare come true.

I had to have a whole lot of help. And in order to beat the booze, I had to drink a whole lot of coffee and smoke a whole lot of cigarettes. There was no other way I could possibly do it. I could only take this on one step at a time. And barely that some days. Some days, it was more like one tiptoe at a time.

Sober for about five years, active in a twelve step program, and surrounded by new friends, I finally began to come down off the walls some. Even though I was still pretty much riddled with tensions, I had this new self-confidence, this new hope that maybe I could do something right after all. So I decided to quit smoking.

That was almost harder than giving up the drinks. It was way, way, way hard. The only way I could do it was to go for about forty-nine walks around the block every day— every time I got the urge in other words. They didn't have patches and nicotine gum back then. We had to go cold turkey.

Well, if you think being without booze brings you face to face with a nightmare, try being without smokes. Never again, I told myself. Those cigarettes had been my front line defense when it came to stress and worry, and without them I didn't even know what to do with myself. I felt all the time like just crawling out of my skin. So, naturally, alongside the walking, I also started eating.

Well, first I gained about forty pounds—that took me a year—and then I had a personal crisis and started smoking again. At least I didn't start drinking too! So I was sober, anyway. But now fat and smoky.

Does this story have you spinning? It did me! Every time I began to get one thing halfway under control, another cropped up. And round and round it went.

Determined to quit the smoking I went at it again full tilt. This time I started running around the block instead of walking. It wasn't because I loved running. Believe me. It was because I finally figured out that if I could just exhaust myself enough, I'd settle down and the craving would go away for a while.

On I went, not drinking and not smoking and not eating, at least when I was running, and consequently, running and running! Around the block I flew. Between the cartons of ice cream that is. The neighbors probably thought I was wacko. I was.

Nowadays, I believe that every life has an unexpected miracle or two in it, a turning point that just arrives, and changes everything that follows. Back then, I didn't believe any such thing. But the turning point came for me anyway on the day I met my neighbor. Nancy was a quiet miracle, for sure. One that kind of snuck up on me. But even so, there she was.

Depending on your personality type, you may not get this, but the miraculous thing about Nancy was that she understood moderation. In fact, she was moderate by nature! Completely in touch with herself, she ate when she was hungry, slept when she was tired, laughed often, relaxed easily, and took on life in a true spirit of gratitude. She wasn't overweight, and didn't have a cigarette hanging out of her mouth.

Now I'd grown up in an intense, addictive, unpredictable family. The folks in treatment were like I was—addictive personalities—but just further along in their recovery. The people I picked for friends were like that too. These were the kind of people I felt at home with. They were the most familiar. I had—literally, in all these years—never gotten to know someone who was kind of normal in the intensity department, kind of balanced and happy. I didn't know what it looked like to live that way.

So Nancy was out in her yard pulling weeds one summer day when I sped past her in my running shoes for the umpteenth time. As I pulled up to a panting halt before my gate, she shouted out with a friendly laugh, "Hello, neighbor! You sure run a lot!"

It was an innocent enough comment, but it made me mad. "So what?" I shouted back.

I couldn't believe it. Nancy actually looked hurt, and then she actually apologized! "I'm sorry," she said, sounding like she really meant it. "I just notice you run a lot."

Her face was so kind. I walked toward her. We began to talk. And in the days that followed, we got to know one another better and better. But not how you might think.

Nancy wasn't so interested in all my addictive behavior stuff or my sordid history in a crummy family. She liked to talk about books, and movies, and sometimes recipes or what happened that day at work. In other words, normal stuff!

At first, to be honest, she seemed a little boring. But I also noticed how calm I felt in her presence. Something in my body just relaxed when I talked to her. Somehow, very gently, the slow miracle of her influence began to flow in my direction. I began to learn from her, even though she didn't presume to be teaching me anything at all.

One day, when I told her that I wished I could lose some weight, she didn't analyze it or turn it into some deep complicated issue. She just said, "I hear Weight Watchers works," and went on to something else. So I went to Weight Watchers. And wouldn't you know, it worked.

Do I have worries? Do I have problems? Troubles? Sure I do. For one thing, I have an addictive personality that probably won't ever go away completely. I still have trouble finding the middle of any road, and sometimes need help just plain staying on the road in the first place without falling into a ditch. I like answers to come quickly, often more quickly than what's realistic.

But nowadays I also like to eat when I'm hungry, sleep when I'm tired, walk when I feel like walking, run when I feel like running, and even plunk down in an easy chair every so often too. I like to relax after work, go outside on a sunny day, lean across the backyard fence, and talk to my neighbor about books, or movies, or recipes.

You may not believe it, but I'm getting normal! Nancy taught me about that, bless her heart.

Mary Kay

Every life holds that which only a miracle can cure.

Sue Bender

WAY 5:

Imagine the Worst and Work from There

LET US BE OF GOOD CHEER,
REMEMBERING THAT THE MISFORTUNES
HARDEST TO BEAR
ARE OFTEN THOSE THAT NEVER COME.

Amy Lowell

Long ago and far away, in a time and place that only the old ones can remember, there lived a poor young woman named Katrina, whose life was riddled with trouble.

She lived with her husband and five children in the tiniest of huts, so that the children had to sleep head to toe like sardines in a single bed, while she and her husband lay in a heap of hay on the floor. The roof leaked terribly, and on rainy days, drops of water constantly plunked down on their heads.

With no room for a table, everyone had to eat their porridge each morning by holding a bowl in their lap.

When porridge was to be had, that is. Sometimes, they only had a crust of bread, and the children wept with hunger.

In the yard outside, held in by a torn and wobbly fence, were several cows, goats, and chickens. They were always mooing, shuffling, clucking, and snorting, waking Katrina up too early in the morning, and requiring more care and attention than she could possibly provide.

At last she walked to visit the Wise Woman at the end of the lane. "Our life is horrible," she cried out. "We're all on top of one another. There isn't even room to move, much less clean or play!" She went on from there, describing her troubled life in detail, until she was spent. "Wise Woman," she said at last, "what should I do?"

"Do you promise you'll follow my instructions exactly?" the Wise Woman asked.

"Yes, yes, of course. Anything to get me out of this!" came Katrina's desperate reply.

"All right then," the Wise Woman continued. "I want you to go home again and ask your neighbors if all their children can come stay in your house for a while. After you have done that, I want you to bring all the animals into your house with you as well—the cows, the goats, and even the chickens. Live under those conditions for a week, then come back and see me again."

Katrina could not believe her ears, but after all, she had promised. She went home and did exactly as the Wise Woman had instructed, enduring somehow what surely must have been the messiest, smelliest, most crowded, most discouraging and difficult week of her life.

After seven full days of this living hell, she dragged herself back down the lane to the Wise Woman's home. She had chicken feathers stuck to her hair, and her dress was torn and tattered, dirty with spilled porridge and animal dung. Her stomach was rumbling with hunger, her eyes bleary from lack of sleep, but she had achieved her task.

"I've spent the week as you asked," she told the Wise Woman, yawning widely even as she spoke. "Twenty people and fourteen animals in our little hut. What next?"

"Now send all your visitors out again: animals back to their yard and neighbor children back to their parents," the Wise Woman said. "Then come back to see me again in one week."

Katrina did exactly as she was told. One week later, she stood dutifully before the Wise Woman's hut, ready to report.

"And how is your life now?" the Wise Woman asked.

"My life has somehow become wonderful!" Katrina exclaimed. "Our home feels so spacious now! And most days there is enough porridge for all of us. And the children all fit into one big bed, so that I can cover them up at night and give them each a kiss. And there are no cows chewing on the hay that my husband and I sleep on, and no chickens squawking in my ear. I tell you, it's a miracle to me, my life has never seemed better."

Such a life it is! Poor Katrina had to experience—in Amy Lowell's words—"those misfortunes hardest to bear" in order to finally manage her fear and worry. For most of us, thankfully, such worst case scenarios are "those which never come." But that doesn't stop us from worrying about them!

I call it the "what if" syndrome, and it can be a major worry-generator. Things are hard enough already, but we find ourselves living in fear that they might get even worse. Floating out there on the horizon of our consciousness are truly frightening imagined scenarios, all beginning with the words "what if."

What if this nagging pain in my chest is a heart attack about to happen?

What if this unopened letter from work turns out to be a discharge notice?

What if my teenager gets in a car crash?

What if I can't answer any of the questions on this test and fail?

We try to block these scary scenarios out. It seems that focusing on them too much might actually make them come true. We try to avoid thinking about them, not wanting to give them any power. But they hover, and they keep coming back at us, at quiet moments or when we've let our guard down. And we find ourselves worrying, and worrying, and worrying.

Imagining the absolute worst, welcoming those fearsome scenarios instead of doing the opposite, then processing them, and even fleshing them out fully in our imagination is a strategy I credit to Dale Carnegie who wrote one of the first books about worry back in the 1940s. According to Carnegie, if you can delve into your deepest fears and learn to master them, your worries decrease significantly, and you grow in confidence, calm, and even readiness.

In my hospice chaplaincy work, I meet with individuals who have recently been told that their illness is terminal. Especially at first, to learn that the time has come for them to face death itself can be one of the most frightening junctures in a person's life. I have learned a great deal by working alongside my team member, a nurse, Jerry, who is quite intentional about asking his patients, "What are you most afraid of? What are you most worried about?"

Sometimes they cannot answer him right away, for the worry and fear are whirling around within them like a tornado, and they simply cannot find words. But Jerry cares about the question because he knows that its answer is tied to their comfort and their capacity to cope with worry. He will ask again or in another way until they can tell him. Somewhere in their psyche, they carry a "worst case scenario," a picture of their own future that is almost too terrifying to contemplate. He wants them to name it.

Sometimes—in fact, often—patients will tell him at last, "It's not death I fear, it's pain. I just don't know if I can deal with all this if I have to go through a lot of pain." Jerry helps them get even more specific, by asking gently, "Pain where? What kind of pain?"

As soon as they have imagined the worst pain and given its description, Jerry is in a position to help them cope with it. He will describe in great detail the several strategies and medications available to help them. He will tell them about initial symptoms, so that they can identify when their pain might be building. He'll teach them about what to do, when to do it, who to call, and how to proceed in the face of pain.

By the time Jerry is done, his patients have become pain experts. They have faced their worst fear with his help and worked from there to master it, to learn literally everything they can to deal with it well. Pain, then, becomes much less threatening for them. They no longer lie in bed worrying and worrying about it. In large part, their final days have been freed to focus on other things.

Imagining our worst fears or naming what we most worry about has tremendous liberating power. Once we've imagined and named the worst, we can begin working from there.

FEAR IS A QUESTION: WHAT ARE YOU
AFRAID OF, AND WHY?
JUST AS THE SEED OF HEALTH IS IN
ILLNESS,
OUR FEARS ARE A TREASURE HOUSE OF
SELF-KNOWLEDGE IF WE EXPLORE
THEM.

Marilyn Ferguson

Imagine the Worst and Work from There

The following four exercises are interconnected and are best worked through in order:

- Make a list of the three things you worry about or dread the most. Try not to belabor the list, but instead write down the first three things that float into your mind. Next, prioritize them from 1 to 3, in order of greatest to least amount of worry they cause.

- Take your number one worry and write it across the top of a fresh sheet of paper. Then use your imagination to describe it fully in the form of a worst case scenario. This might take a paragraph or several pages. Let yourself write as much as you need to.

- On yet another sheet of fresh paper, write: What I Can Do to Prepare Myself. Following that, create a list of tasks—every possible act or decision that would prepare you to deal with this scenario. Again, prioritize this list from most important task to least important.

- Work through the list. Even if you never do everything on it, the process itself will likely afford you great release from worry.

LET ME NOT PRAY TO BE SHELTERED FROM DANGERS
BUT TO BE FEARLESS IN FACING THEM.
LET ME NOT BEG FOR THE STILLING OF MY PAIN
BUT FOR THE HEART TO HANDLE IT.

Rabindranath Tagore

Befriending My Worst Fears

One day, during a routine annual physical, my doctor thought she felt some larger-than-usual masses in my uterine area. Following up with ultrasound and then an MRI, she identified a mass growing on my right ovary.

I am a single parent with two children, Josh and Jake, who are twelve and ten years old, respectively. News of this mass sent me into a panic. I couldn't imagine what would happen to my children if something happened to me, and I could barely stand to think about it. What's more, several years ago, I'd lost a dear friend to ovarian cancer, and I could still remember how much she struggled, how long and hard she fought for life before surrendering to death.

The doctor told me that she'd like me to come back for another MRI in three months to see if this mass had grown. She told me it was unlikely that it was cancer, but somehow her words weren't particularly comforting to me. "What percent chance that it's cancer?" I asked.

"Oh, less than ten percent," she responded.

I am sure she was trying to reassure me. But suddenly, ten percent sounded like a huge number to me. It meant that one chance in ten, I'd be dealing with an unthinkable disaster. For three months, I was jittery and on edge. My friends listened kindly to my worries and tried their best to comfort me. To be honest, however, nothing much helped.

The next MRI showed that the mass had grown, but only slightly. My doctor proposed one more three-month interval followed by yet another MRI. "If it has grown more by then," she said, "we'll go ahead with surgery. But try not to worry about this, everything is going to be all right."

Three more months! I could barely stand the thought. Sometimes, when you're deeply worried about something, sweeping reassurances just don't make a dent in it. They are simply less powerful than the worry itself, and far easier to dismiss. This was something I really needed to deal with in a different way.

I had never imagined my own death, which was also my biggest fear. I'd never asked myself what would really happen to my children, my belongings—my whole life. I had never written a will. Never written a living will, for that matter. Never allowed myself to even think that such a thing could happen to our little family. Now it was time.

I forced myself to imagine the worst "what if" of all: that I did have ovarian cancer and would live for months, not years, before dying. I imagined how it would feel, how I'd explain things to Josh and Jake, who I'd ask to care for them and for me in the later phases of illness.

When I faced this "what if" head on, I felt deeply sad, but also—interestingly—more grounded, more prepared for action, than I had since the mass had first been identified. The tasks before me became clear.

I could not afford a lawyer, so I went to the library and checked out a book about writing your own will. Within two weeks, this document was completed and witnessed before a notary public. I could not believe the relief I felt just knowing it was in place.

Next, I contacted the local hospital and obtained two samples of living wills. This involved answering several questions about my wishes for care in case of serious or incapacitating illness, as well as selecting a proxy. I picked a friend and asked her if she'd play that role. She said yes. Next I asked my sister if she'd be there for the kids if anything were to happen to me. She, too, said yes.

I'd never talked to the boys about these things, and didn't know how to begin. After some thought, I decided to bring it up without getting specific and thereby passing on to them my own panic about the ovarian mass. We had a few generic conversations about what would happen if I was ever too sick to care for them. I kept it low key, and they took it in stride. In other words, the topic had been broached. Were I to have ovarian cancer, they would not be caught completely off guard.

By the time those next three months were up, I was still fairly worried about my health, but feeling much better in general, and much more in control of my own fate. I had done just about all I could to prepare for a worst-case scenario. Letting go was a reasonable next step. The mass had grown again, and I had to face surgery. Thank goodness all my affairs were in order.

After all that, it turned out to be a benign mass! But in six months, I had learned some valuable lessons in responsibility, courage, and good self-care. Hopefully, I will never again avoid facing my worst fears. I've learned to trust the seemingly paradoxical truth that facing them to the best of my ability frees me from them as well.

Nancy Solomon

BE PREPARED

The Girl and Boy Scout Motto

Big Dog

One day when I was a four-year-old kid, I noticed a German shepherd roaming around our neighborhood. Probably my mom had told me never to go up to strange dogs, but her lesson evidently was forgotten as my curiosity got the better of me. So I walked over to pat him. He was a great big dog, I remember, with a thick, matted coat of fur, and, so I thought at the time, kind and friendly eyes.

Well, he did let me pet him for a while, and I innocently thought his low growls were just greetings. Then when I turned my back to leave, he attacked me from behind, biting the backs of my legs right through my jeans, growling, grabbing my arm in his jaws, and shaking me like a doll.

I was screaming with fear and, just as a neighbor came out to help, the dog took off. My neighbor carried me into his house and called the police who must have called the dogcatcher next because within minutes both arrived.

They scoured the neighborhood until they found the dog, which had gotten out of someone's yard a few days earlier and wandered around, probably afraid and on the defensive ever since. I had to go to the hospital and get several stitches in my legs where the skin was punctured and torn. And I remember a policeman taking photos of my wounds for their records.

Everyone was really nice to me. The folks at the hospital were soothing and gentle. My mom and dad didn't scold me at all. And my grandpa who lived with us and was really good with all animals taught me some safety tips: back away from a strange dog instead of turning away and always avoid looking one straight in the eye. It turned out that his lessons were pretty unnecessary because from then on I was terrified of and avoided not just big dogs, but all dogs. It didn't matter what size or shape, friendly face or fierce one, I stayed clear. I crossed the street if one was headed my way. Even the sight of a dog made me sick to my stomach with fear.

This may sound small, but actually it interfered with my life a lot. Dogs, being "man's best friend," tend to turn up all over the place. When I wasn't worried about an actual dog, I was worried about running into one, no matter where I went. This went on for about ten years.

Then something else happened. My grandfather had to move into a nursing home. He'd lived with us for as long as I could remember, but had gotten too sick and weak to stay home anymore. I was so close to him and so used to having him around that I rode my bike over to visit him after school fairly often.

At first Grandpa seemed really lonely there, no matter how much we visited. After he began to get to know some other people, though, it got easier. What he talked about most was some volunteer who came to visit him each week. The guy's name, he said, was Blacky. Well, I did think that was sort of an odd name. But it didn't matter to me who this Blacky was as long as he helped my grandpa be happy.

Some time around the holidays, I noticed Grandpa's Christmas card from Blacky tacked up on his bulletin board. It was a photograph of Blacky himself in a Santa hat next to a great big decorated tree. That's when I realized that Blacky wasn't a person at all, but a dog—one of those volunteer dogs that are brought to nursing homes and hospitals to cheer people up. What's more, I could tell from the photo: Blacky was gigantic.

I started to get really jumpy about going to visit. The old familiar feeling in the pit of my stomach came right back even when I thought about going over to the nursing home. What if I ran into this dog in the hall, or even worse, in Grandpa's room? What if he got protective of Grandpa and attacked me? I knew none of this made sense. I knew that any dog allowed into a nursing home would have to be well trained and gentle, and also be leashed to the person in charge of him. But even so.

Grandpa noticed that I wasn't coming around as often as before. "How come you're not visiting me much these days?" he asked one day. Well, he knew me pretty well, my grandpa did, and he saw that as soon as the question was out of his mouth, my eyes shot over to the photo of Blacky in the Santa hat.

He understood right away. "Oh, the dog thing," he said. "Say, what's the worst thing you think could happen, anyway?"

The fears and worries tumbled out. What if the dog was not just huge but also fierce? What if it attacked? What if it hurt me? I got jittery just saying the words.

Grandpa was quiet. And then he said, "Well, what if those things did happen? For one thing, I'd be right here. I wouldn't let anything hurt you, Randy, and certainly not Blacky! Who, by the way, wouldn't hurt a flea anyway. Even though I do admit he's a pretty big guy. You'd love him, Randy, I know you would."

I stared at Grandpa, weak and frail in the bed, and thought about how he'd never be able to protect me even if he wanted to. "But what if you can't stop him?" I asked, knowing even as I said it how irrational it must have sounded.

Grandpa didn't laugh at me or anything. He helped me think it through. After all, he pointed out, it was a nursing home, and there was a whole staff there to help if anything went wrong. And then he told me all about Blacky, his size, his personality, and even his owner. "Come visit me next Thursday after school, Randy," he went on. "I want you to meet him. He's my friend. He'll be here waiting for you."

All Thursday during school, I fought off nausea. Couldn't eat lunch. Had trouble concentrating. At last the final bell rang. It was time. I got on my bike and set off, filled with trepidation. Anyone but Grandpa, and I would never be doing this.

When I got to Grandpa's room, the door was just slightly ajar. Gathering all my courage, I peeked in quietly and saw that Blacky had already arrived. There was the most gigantic dog I had ever seen. He looked to be about the size of a small horse, except I couldn't really tell for sure because Blacky was lying on the rug with all four feet sticking up in the air, letting Grandpa rub his tummy. And tied in a hank of hair on the top of his head, a little blue bow. Pink tongue hanging out. His owner—a kind looking elderly lady about half his size—was sitting on a chair next to him, holding his leash.

I took one cautious step into the room.

Blacky curled his ears, clown-like, and thumped his tail to smile at me.

Grandpa laughed.

I took another step.

And another.

And all the rest is history.

I'll always be grateful to Blacky for showing me that I didn't need to worry so much about dogs. And I'll always be grateful to Grandpa for encouraging me to meet Blacky.

But I also know, deep inside, that neither one of them would have been able to help if I hadn't been willing to look into the darkest corners of my own fear and face what I saw there.

Randy Ferguson

LET ME ASSERT MY FIRM BELIEF THAT THE ONLY THING WE HAVE TO FEAR IS FEAR ITSELF.

Franklin D. Roosevelt

WAY 6 :

Put Your Worry to Work

IT IS BETTER TO WEAR OUT THAN TO
RUST OUT.

Frances Willard

I came up with the phrase "work your worry off" from the woman whose story eventually became the last one in this chapter. Believe me, she's someone who's had a lot of experience. You'll meet her, eventually. But first, meet this young man:

One bright and sunlit morning, long ago and far away, a youth walking along the seashore noticed that the tide had left the sands covered with millions of stranded starfish, all of them struggling for life. He began immediately to pick them up, one by one, and throw them back into the ocean.

A much older man approached and, witnessing the same scene, asked the youth what he thought he was doing.

"I am concerned for these starfish and I'm trying to rescue them from certain death," came the reply.

This launched the older man into a short but pointed lecture. Laughing bitterly, he said, "But look, there are millions of them here. Do you really think that throwing them back, one by one, is going to make any difference?"

With a shy smile, the younger man picked up a starfish and threw it as far as he could into the salty water. Looking his elder straight in the eye, he answered, "Well, I bet it just made a difference to that one."

Whenever something is worrying you, you have a choice. You can put your worry in the service of fear and anxiety and frustration, or you can put it to work. The older man in the story chose the former; the younger man the latter.

Surely, as the story went, millions of starfish died. Thanks to the young man though, some did not. But that's not even a true story, you may be thinking. It may be amazing, but it's also just a fairy tale! Correct.

The following story, which brings us to a similar conclusion, is both amazing and true. It comes to us, translated and paraphrased here, from the memoirs of Miroslav Holub.

The young lieutenant of a small Hungarian detachment in the Alps sent a reconnaissance unit out on a mission into the icy wasteland. Immediately following their departure, the sky filled with heavy clouds. It began to snow, and then continued to snow heavily for two more days. The longer this unit remained gone, the more their lieutenant suffered. It was his overriding worry that he had sent his own troops into certain death.

Surprisingly, on the next day, the full unit returned. Not a single man had been lost. Proud, thrilled, and most of all relieved, their concerned lieutenant had a thousand questions for them. Where had they been? How had they made their way? What had they done to survive?

"We too considered ourselves lost," one began. "We had actually already gathered ourselves into a huddle and prepared to wait for the end when one of us found a map in his pocket. That calmed us down considerably. We pitched camp, lasted out the snowstorm, and then used the map to discover our bearings and return. Here we are!"

The lieutenant borrowed this remarkable map and took a good, long look at it. Astounded, he turned to his men and said, "But this is not a map of the Alps. It is a map of the Pyrenees."

Again, you almost always have a choice: You can put your worry in the service of fear and anxiety, or you can put it to work. As this second story suggests, it may not matter so much how you put it to work—wrong map, wrong strategy, or wrong plan. More important is that you simply turn the energy of it into action. That alone can make all the difference.

Please don't confuse this strategy with being addicted to work! It's not the same as working in an addictive fashion: that is, using work to block worry out or enter an exhausted oblivion. It is an honest attempt to respond directly and energetically but not fanatically to that which concerns you deeply.

Granted, when worry gets a good hold on the human heart, it will often transform our best intentions into hopelessness. Hopelessness, in turn, can move us to extremes: sometimes paralysis and sometimes impulsive overachievement.

"Putting worry to work" is different from either extreme. It means approaching a scenario boldly; responding to it directly—and proportionately—with action, motion, movement. It is a straightforward and uncomplicated strategy, perhaps the simplest of all those presented in this book. Which is not to say that the simplest things are necessarily the easiest.

Suffice it to say that this strategy precludes lengthy explanation. In fact, lengthy explanation—or any sort of convoluted internal dialogue whatsoever—is exactly what inhibits it. It's one of those things you just have to go do. Throwing fear to the winds, along with all your clutching desires for control or perfection, just go do it.

WHEN YOU'RE FRIGHTENED DON'T SIT STILL, KEEP ON DOING SOMETHING. THE ACT OF DOING WILL GIVE YOU BACK YOUR COURAGE.

Grace Ogot

Put Your Worry to Work

- First, pick one worry that tends to paralyze you or send you into frenetic overdrive, perhaps because of hopelessness, discouragement, or lack of knowing how to handle it. Put on your brainstorming cap, adjust your sense-of-humor goggles, set your stopwatch or kitchen timer for five minutes, and "Go!" See if you can generate at least ten direct, action-oriented ways to respond to this worry. Write them down in a list. You may find that in order to meet your deadline, you have to get pretty silly. Set the list aside.

- Next, several hours or days later, look over the list again and pick out three actions you wrote down. Promise yourself that before the week is out, you will try out all three of them. To make this exercise more vigorous, try out five—or even all ten!

- Close your eyes and imagine that each worrisome thought you have is a starfish on the beach. In a day, will you find ten starfish there, or a thousand, or a million? All day long, whenever you notice a worrisome thought, pick it up, and "toss it back into the water," so to speak. Say to yourself as you send it sailing, "Goodbye to another one!"

- If people were cars, our worries would be like crude oil that we would need to change into useable fuel or gasoline. Think about the last time that you felt truly "stalled" by worry and exhausted or anxious because of it. How did you handle the situation? How might you have changed the worry into fuel—that is, fuel that had the power to get you going again and send you moving along?

I DON'T WASTE TIME ASKING, "AM I
DOING IT RIGHT?"

I JUST ASK, "AM I DOING IT?"

Georgette Mosbacher

Worry Vs. Ludefisk: Which Will Win?

Margaret, who is almost ninety years old, had lost much in the past year. Her husband died. Then her children moved her into an assisted living facility near them. Having them close by was important, but it put Margaret over an hour from her old neighborhood and the beloved Lutheran church where she had grown up, gotten married, baptized all her babies, and been in a faith circle for years.

A few times, she had tried driving back to church on Sunday. Gotten lost once. Gotten into a minor accident once. Had her seatbelt on, luckily. Her children begged her to give up the car, and she did. No husband, no house, no car, no church. And then, the diagnosis: pancreatic cancer.

As her brand new hospice chaplain, I sat with her in the tiny living room of her new apartment. She told me about what her church did at this time of year. There was a luncheon, and all the "ladies"—as she called them—came. All the men, in aprons, served. There was a program, and the minister led everyone in carols. Best of all, though, were those same Norwegian foods that had signaled Christmas to her for as long as she could remember: lefse and cardamom bread, boiled potatoes in butter, lingonberries, and of course, ludefisk with clarified butter or mustard sauce or white sauce—you got to choose.

Not this year. It was too far, and she was too sick.

"I could take you," I said.

"If you could do that," she said, her eyes alight with anticipation, "then you could stay for lunch with me and my friends."

As the day of the luncheon approached, I began to worry about liability. What if she fell on the church steps? What if she had a stroke in my care? What if a surge of unbearable pain came on her? She had already fallen more than once because of that, and yet still refused to use the wheelchair we had gotten her, preferring her cane instead.

Worries tormented me. This journey seemed high risk. After all, this was a woman's well-being, her life. Torn and knowing that if I were to consult someone I might be told that transporting patients was not allowed, I spoke not a word to anyone, and then felt uncomfortable, sneaky, somehow in violation of something.

The morning of the luncheon arrived. At our staff meeting that day—literally minutes before I was to go pick up Margaret—the topic of patient transportation came up. I learned that as staff we were not ever to transport patients ourselves and that our organization did not have insurance to cover it.

I got into my car and began the hour-long drive to Margaret's apartment not knowing what to do and pretty much immobilized by misgivings. On the freeway I came up behind a taxi with a phone number painted on its side, and called the driver. I asked him how much a trip such as this would cost. "Oh, about $80." he said. "One way, that is."

"Thanks anyway." I hung up.

Next I tried the number of my best friend Marie for a consult. No answer. Finally, I called Margaret herself. She sounded so excited, so happy. "My friend has been here, helping me with my hair," she half shouted into the phone. "And I have on my Christmas outfit, and. . . ."

"But Margaret," I said, interrupting her. "Listen. There's a problem. I'm not supposed to drive patients

anywhere. Our insurance doesn't cover it. But I'm coming
out there to be with you anyway, and I'm just so sorry this
had to happen. I feel terrible about it, but those are the
rules."

I anticipated that she would be heartbroken. Not so.
She stepped right over my news as though it was a small
barricade in the road upon which she was traveling most
joyously toward Jerusalem. Or perhaps she hadn't heard
me—after all, she did wear two hearing aids.

"What color is your car?" she wanted to know next.
"Red, you say? Now don't you park it. Just pull it up in the
circle drive, and I'll be waiting."

When I pulled into the circle drive, Margaret was
indeed all ready. More than ready. Her hair was done
beautifully, a snowy white arrangement of waves and
curls, and she had on sparkly red and green clip earrings.
Her cane was tucked under her arm. No wheelchair in
sight.

Not sure what to do—but knowing it had to be
something—I simply took a wild guess at the right choice.
I helped her into my car. "Look, Margaret," I said, before
turning the ignition. "Since I'm not supposed to be doing
this, perhaps you'd sign a little note releasing our hospice
program from liability. Kind of like when your kids went
on field trips."

Though we both suspected that such a note wouldn't
really hold up in the event of an accident, she wrote it out
immediately and signed it with a flourish, adding, "But in
a way it is more fun, more of an adventure, really, because
we're breaking the rules." She had heard me on the phone.
She had understood all along. While I'd been immobilized
by worry, she had been mobilized by it.

It was a wild trip, to be sure. We got lost on the way to

the church because she'd forgotten how to get there. But I had a map, so we found our way again and arrived on time. She did almost fall going up the church steps, but luckily caught herself, and when she walked through the door, a swarm of ladies just her age circled around her, patting her cheeks tenderly, kissing her, saying how good—how very good and special—it was to have her there. And she kept introducing me to them. "This is my hospice chaplain," she'd say, and then they'd swarm all over me and pat my cheeks, too. And then we were seated in our chairs, and sang *Hark, the Herald Angels Sing, First Noel, Angels We Have Heard on High.* The pastor said grace, and the men in aprons came out with their laden platters.

It was over the ludefisk, I think, that I finally relaxed and felt the worry fall away. Because of the look on her face, because of the vast amount of love and tenderness that surrounded her in this very moment, I finally reached my own peace. Maybe I'd made a good choice, maybe a bad one. But no matter what happened next—now or on the way home—it was all worth it.

This was exactly where we belonged, Margaret and I, and nowhere else in the world.

JoAnn LaBraign

IT ISN'T WHAT HAPPENS TO YOU, IT'S WHAT YOU DO ABOUT WHAT HAPPENS TO YOU, THAT CONTROLS THE QUALITY OF YOUR LIFE.

Susan Mendenhall

Wearing Worry Down Until It's Gone

Sometimes, when I watch young kids these days—and by that I mean anyone fifty or younger—I have to wonder if they know anything about handling the hard stuff at all. No disrespect intended, but nowadays they turn to talk shows, self-help books, therapy this, and therapy that. It's no wonder to me that everyone's a bundle of nerves.

When we were young, there was a war going on. The people we loved most—our fathers, brothers, husbands, and neighbors—were being shipped off in great numbers to fight against a crazy man: Adolf Hitler. We said good-bye, not knowing if we would ever see them again. There was no Internet, no e-mail. There were no satellite news reports from some other side of the globe. No sir, after we'd sent them off, all we could do next was hope from the bottom of our hearts to get a letter from them now and then, or to hear Churchill bring us good news on a radio broadcast.

Talk about worry. Almost everyone I knew was worried—every day—about a loved one. It was learn how to handle it or bust. Some of us did bust. Couldn't take the pressure, that is. Ended up with drinking problems or hospitalized for nervous breakdowns. But most of us—with one another's help—learned how to endure a very large amount of daily worry and fret. And our main tactic back then was this: we worked our worry off.

Since few people these days seem to take that approach, let me explain it. Say you were worried about your little brother over there in France or Italy, maybe on the front lines, maybe flying a bomber plane, or out on a Navy vessel. There wasn't much you could do for him. He was just so far away. But still you found yourself thinking about him all the time. To sit and stew in that was certain doom.

So you'd find a way—just some way—to do something that might help. If you could just keep busy making some contribution, no matter how small, you found you felt much better.

Some of us wrote letters to loved ones every day. We never knew if most of those letters reached their destination, but it was a relief to try anyway. Some of us formed church groups that worked for the American Red Cross. We rolled bandages, made up first aid kits, and did all kinds of small tasks that kept us busy, had us working alongside each other, and made us feel useful. Some of us helped out the families that suffered because of a missing soldier. That could mean collecting clothes for kids, bringing over food, or keeping an extra eye out for a widow that might need something but would never say so.

Some of us grew victory gardens. Some of us bought war bonds. A lot of us joined the work force, to keep our households going. Some of us shared our rations, so that the ones who needed gas or coffee or something else the most would be sure to get it.

And when the day had ended, if we were still worried, then we'd get down on our knees in prayer. "Don't ever tell me there's nothing you can do," my mother would say. "Even if you're dumb, deaf, and blind, even if you're sick in bed or lost in the woods, you can always pray. You can always turn to God. Just think," she'd add, "if David had decided not to fling that rock at Goliath. Don't talk to me about hopelessness."

Some of our men came home safe and sound. Many did not. Determined as we were, there was much that we had no power over in those difficult days. But we knew how to get through.

We just kept working at it and working at it—working our worry off, until we were too tired to worry anymore.

Edythe Olson

I WILL ACT AS THOUGH WHAT I DO MAKES A DIFFERENCE.

William James

WAY 7:

Practice Re-Framing

DO NOT WORRY ABOUT WHAT YOU WILL
EAT, OR WHAT YOU WILL WEAR . . .
CONSIDER THE LILIES OF THE FIELD, AND
HOW THEY GROW. . . .

Jesus of Nazareth

You may recognize these words. They are the words of Jesus, speaking to his followers. At first glance, they conjure up for most of us an idyllic gathering of young and old alike, gathered around their beloved Master, listening to his teachings amidst a field of beautiful flowers.

The truth is quite different. The people Jesus offered these words to were not in an idyllic situation at all. They were struggling with oppression by Roman rulers, deprivation, and anxiety for their lives. They were hungry, afraid, discouraged, and about to give up. So why in the world would he tell them, at such a time, to look at a bunch of lilies?

The answer: because he was re-framing their situation for them. Re-framing begins with the understanding that your situation, no matter how worrisome or frightening it may seem, is often in large part the result of how you choose to see it. In the same way that a photographer can take snapshots of something from a wide range of different angles, so too can we look at any single situation from several different perspectives. Things are not as they are, but as we are.

Jesus was not telling his people to ignore the fact that they were hungry and poor and discouraged. He was just telling them to look at things from a different perspective, then to remember that, even in the midst of their suffering, they were precious to a loving God. Jesus gently pointed out to them that even the lilies were in God's care, and they as God's people were too—even more so. He was inviting them to focus the lenses of their understanding not on anxiety, but on trust—trust that God would uphold them. The lilies were a symbol, an illustration of the lesson being taught.

Now I invite you to shift the focus of your own lens from two thousand years ago, where Jesus stood with his people, to the present day, and the work of a man named Edmund Bourne. In his excellent text, *The Anxiety and Phobia Workbook*, Bourne helps us work with re-framing in more contemporary terms. He posits that there are four anxiety-producing ways that we tend to frame our experience. If we can become aware of these ways, we will have much greater capacity to re-frame our experience or look at it from a more helpful, hopeful angle.

He labels the first less-than-useful way of framing experience "The Worrier" way. When we come at life from this perspective, we tend to anticipate the worst, overestimate the odds of something bad happening, and create images of potential failure. Our most common expression is "What if. . . ." Let's say you're about to make a speech. If you're operating out of the Worrier perspective, you're saying to yourself, "What if I forget my lines? What if I stutter? What if they laugh at me?" Predictably, your anxiety will only increase.

Bourne calls a second troublesome perspective, "The Critic." When we use this angle to view experience, we constantly focus on our own flaws, limitations, and mistakes. We tend to bombard ourselves with phrases like, "Why can't I ever get it right?" or "How stupid!" or "What a disappointment or failure or idiot (or, insert your own descriptor here) I am!" If you approach that same speech from the Critic perspective, you might be saying to yourself, "I'm just not good enough, because . . . " or "I know I'll fail, because. . . . "

Bourne's third anxiety-producing perspective is called "The Victim." When we see life from this angle, we focus primarily on insurmountable obstacles, and the belief that nothing will ever change. We tend to say to ourselves things like, "I just can't . . . " or "I'll never be able to. . . . " If you see life often through this angle, you'll probably never agree to give a public speech in the first place.

Bourne's fourth and last problematic perspective is that of "The Perfectionist." Similar to the Critic perspective, this one generates worry and anxiety by constantly goading us to be the absolute best and to have everything under control. We become intolerant of all mistakes or setbacks, and often use the phrase "I should. . . . " Facing the speech from this perspective, you might be thinking, "Now I should be on top of this," or "I should have more control over this!" Naturally, when you allow yourself no room for imperfection, worrying skyrockets.

The good news is this: re-framing is possible in all four situations. We do have the power to shift our angle, move our lens, and see life from more constructive and hopeful perspectives. It isn't necessarily easy or automatic but, without a doubt, it can be done.

Shifting to a new perspective may be most difficult if you've held the old one for a long time. It is human nature to become almost comfortable with a certain angle on life, even when that angle makes things hard in several other ways. But it can be done. Jesus would not have called upon his people to notice those beautiful lilies so long ago had he not believed deeply in their ability to do so, even in the midst of their suffering.

> IN SHORT, YOU ARE LARGELY
> RESPONSIBLE FOR HOW YOU FEEL.
>
> *Edmund Bourne*

Practice Re-Framing

- Reflect upon your preferred angle regarding present concerns. Do you tend toward being:

- The Worrier—"What if . . ."

- The Critic—"Why can't I ever get it right?"

- The Victim—"I'll never be able to . . . "

- The Perfectionist—"I should have more control over this!"

- If one of these names does not fit, what name would you give the angle you tend to use? What phrases or thoughts cue you to the fact that you are using it? Reflect on how your worry-angle has stood in the way of joy and even accomplishment.

- Pick one instance in which you acted like The Worrier, or The Critic, or The Victim, or The Perfectionist. Try to re-frame the situation so that you could have shaped the experience to be positive and energizing.

- For one week, keep a log of those inner worry-voices. If you tend toward the Worrier, each evening log all the Worrier statements that buzzed in your brain that day. Then note how you handled what the Worrier was whispering, or maybe shouting, at you. If you re-framed your perspective, note that too and end the entry with an Alleluia.

- Practice "catching" yourself using a preferred but less-than-constructive angle. This may take some practice, as our perspectives are often deeply engrained. When you do catch yourself, however, "talk back" to yourself—and in this way re-frame the situation. For example, if you notice that you are about to turn down an invitation to a party because of an internal voice that is whispering, "No one would like me anyway," talk back then and there! Say to yourself, "That is just my Victim perspective. I am as likeable as the next person, and I can do this."

- Affirmations prove especially helpful when it comes to re-framing. Select an affirmation for the day, one that will help you put a different angle on your worries. Say it to yourself ten times upon rising, several times throughout the day, and ten times more at bedtime. Keep it short and punchy. Some examples of affirmations:

- I am becoming less worried every day.
- I trust myself.
- It's all right to make mistakes.
- I know I can do it.

I'VE DISCOVERED I ALWAYS HAVE
CHOICES, AND SOMETIMES IT'S ONLY A
CHOICE OF ATTITUDE.

Judith Knowlton

Keep On Truckin'

I'd been an over the road truck driver for more than thirty years when my back pain got too bad to keep working. By the time I quit and had to go on disability, I was in sorry shape, that's for sure. My pain was chronic, continuous, and horrible. They couldn't find a medication to touch it, and then after a while half the docs began to think it was all in my head. But in the meantime I became addicted to a strong painkiller. In other words, things were a mess.

Until you experience chronic, deep pain, you can't imagine how horrible, how all-consuming it is, how much it makes you want to scream, howl, weep, or crawl out of your skin. It can louse up your sleep, your wage earning capacity, your marriage, everything. Talk about worry. Talk about stress. It got so all I could think about was the pain. Pain in the morning when I got up, pain all day, and pain all night.

Finally I ended up in a chronic pain clinic. It definitely had some good things about it. For the first time since my real troubles began, for example, I was with some other people who couldn't sit through an hour in their chairs either, who understood what I was going through because they were going through some version of it too. Let me tell you, no one in that group thought it was "all in my head." What an insult that is when doctors say that. I mean, so what! Pain is pain. Just because they can't figure out where it comes from, why should they blame my head?

Anyway, it was such a relief to be understood and to not be called crazy. But there were definitely some hard parts too. For example, Doc had us do some exercises that I thought were really silly at first. For one of these he had us all create an image of our pain in our heads and tell the group about it. Well I'm not exactly a dream-up and talk-about-it kinda guy. But Doc just let me listen to the others at first until I got used to the idea. And to tell the truth it did get interesting.

One lady in our group said her pain was like a cruel slave master with a gigantic whip, and she could never get out of its sight. It just kept lashing her and lashing her. And another guy said his pain was like a monster, the kind from those old Godzilla movies, and it killed him every day. Then every night while he slept, he came back to life, and the thing killed him again the next day. These were all images I could understand. I suppose if you haven't had chronic pain, they might sound a little extreme.

Finally I was the only one who hadn't done the exercise. Doc asked me one last time if I wanted to give it a try, and

I just took a shot at it. Started talking. I told the group that my pain was like a vicious wildcat, a hungry one with mean eyes and sharp teeth. It constantly attacked me in the small of my back. Dug its teeth into the flesh there and shook its head, and all I could do was flop back and forth like a rag doll. It actually fed on my back, gouging out my guts, and making me bleed and bleed. I could never heal because it just kept tearing and tearing at me. And I was too weak to reach around and grab it, and it was going to kill me eventually.

Nobody laughed at me, and when I looked around the group after finishing they all looked sad, like they wished they could help me. And I really surprised myself. I noticed that I was crying. Me! The big guy! Doc told me I did a good job.

The next exercises got harder and harder, but all of us were getting more and more confident in ourselves too. The overall process was to learn to work with those horrible images in all kinds of ways. Doc called it the holistic approach. We used medication, diet, exercise, group support, education, meditation, yoga, massage, prayer, and anything else Doc, or we, could come up with. Our goal was to change the images from things that managed us, into things we could manage. For me, that meant taming the wildcat. Somehow, changing it from my enemy into my ally.

This took a long, long time. At first it seemed impossible. The wildcat was too vicious, too sneaky. I was too torn apart. But Doc promised I could make at least some progress, and because I trusted him, I set to work.

You won't believe this, coming from a guy like me, but the most helpful exercise for me turned out to be meditation. That's because the pain had made it so I couldn't even think. But a half-hour of meditation in the morning—slowly, over time—not only relaxed me, which let some of the tension out of my back, it also allowed me to begin having some mastery over my own mind again. In a relaxed state, using my imagination, I could begin to change how I wanted to picture that horrible wildcat.

The pain clinic lasted for six months, and those turned out to be the most important six months of my life. I'm not pain free today. The pain is still—always—with me. But now it's not my attacker, it's more like my pet. Wildcat to pussycat, so to speak. If I treat it right, it treats me right too. It makes demands of me, like anything in life, but they're demands I can handle: daily rest and back exercises, quiet meditation time each morning, paying attention to when I'm getting tired. And this so-called pet has also taught me all kinds of life lessons: to accept what I can't change, to be patient, and to stop pushing myself so hard. It has also led me to some great new friends.

If I could pass along one thing to someone who feels like they're trapped in a bad place, it's this: You may not have the power to change what's happening, but you do have the power to change how you look at it. Don't give up, ask for help, and keep on truckin'. You'll get there eventually.

John O'Connor

WHEN ONE DOOR OF HAPPINESS CLOSES, ANOTHER OPENS; BUT OFTEN WE LOOK SO LONG AT THE CLOSED DOOR

THAT WE DO NOT SEE THE ONE THAT

HAS BEEN OPENED. . . .

Helen Keller

Another Way to Look at It

Once, when our second son Evan was only five years old, he and I took a trip to a distant city, and stayed in a large downtown hotel there. Evan had always been our more difficult child, so I was in the habit of watching him a bit more carefully than the others, and I did notice that he was fascinated with the large bank of elevators that took the guests up and down to their rooms. But I did not expect him to slip onto a departing elevator as we stood there together one day. And I was absolutely terrified when the elevator door closed quickly and carried him off.

At first I tried to bring Evan back by pushing the elevator buttons as hard as I could, but that had no effect. It didn't stop a thing. So I dashed to the stairway and began racing after the elevator on foot. This hotel had thirty-five floors and eight elevators in this bank alone. I just could not get myself in sync with the one that had taken Evan away from me. When I dashed up to floor seven, it had passed on to nine. When I arrived breathlessly at nine, it had already taken off for twenty-two. Or had he actually gotten on the other one, the one headed for three? Or the other, now paused at thirty-three? The truth of it, I finally understood with some degree of despair, was that my son had set off on his own and left me behind with little to do but worry myself sick wondering how to get him back.

This kind of worry—the kind that parents feel for their children—is in some ways the most insidious of all. It has to do with how much we love them, and how little we can control them. Part of growing up for them is in fact exactly that task, learning how to break loose from us and live their own lives without our controlling presence to guide and protect their every choice. It's inevitable that our children will eventually do something that worries us terribly, no matter how hard we try to keep them safe and within the sphere of our influence. That's the way growing up happens.

Of course none of this wisdom occurred to me as I sat in the lobby sobbing. I could only picture Evan lost forever in vertical movement, up and down, up and down *ad infinitum*: Evan, stolen by some creepy adult who would hurt him; Evan, frightened and lost in the corner of the elevator; my dear little Evan, my sweet precious boy, out of my reach. It was horrible. I felt guilty and sad and frustrated and ashamed all at once. These feelings indeed made the worry—a worry almost akin to panic—worse.

Finally a man behind the desk in the lobby approached me, a box of Kleenex in his hand, which he held out gingerly. "Here, lady, have one of these," he said. "Is there something the matter? Something I can help you with?" He seemed like a good man to me, and a kind one, and he also had on a uniform. It occurred to me that maybe he really could help me. After all, he had some kind of official role, and he probably had understandings about the elevators that I'd never dream of.

I explained to him that I had lost my five-year-old son on the elevators and been unable to find him for several minutes now. He listened patiently as I told him all the terrible things that could happen and how helpless I felt in the face of them. And then he said to me something simple, yet something that has stayed with me for several years, something I still say to myself when worry about Evan overcomes me. He said, in the gentlest tone of voice, "Lady, there's another way to look at that."

First he told me that this happened fairly regularly, that every so often a child would step unexpectedly onto the elevator and get whisked away, much to the horror of his or her parents. "And it's always the curious ones, always the adventurous ones," he added. "They just can't seem to help themselves. They're probably our country's future airplane pilots, or parachute jumpers, or mountain climbers," he commented with a smile. "But you know what I've learned? What goes up has to come down. And when it comes to elevators, what goes down has to also come up. So if you and I go stand there, and if we wait long enough, I can just about guarantee you that he'll turn up pretty soon. And don't be surprised if he's had the time of his life."

I had often thought about Evan as naughty, disobedient, and resistant to instruction. But I had never thought about him in the positive light this kind man was now describing him: adventurous, curious, and destined for acts of bravery.

Sure enough, after a while, one of the doors swung open, and there was my son. He did look as though he'd had the time of his life! Furthermore, he had evidently charmed everyone he'd ridden with by pushing the buttons for them, blocking the door with his body, and now holding the hand of an elderly woman who had taken it upon herself to return him to the lobby desk.

"I had one just like him, some time ago," she said to me with a twinkle in her eye, passing him off to me. "They can stretch a mother pretty thin, but their spirits are impossible to break. They grow into very admirable adults! But please, just don't ask me where my gray hair came from," she added with a wink.

The truth is, Evan has never changed. He has remained a risk-taker, a daredevil, and an adventurous soul, all the way into adulthood. If I've said it to myself once, during all these years, I've said it to myself a thousand times, whenever he's shown me that particular side of his nature. "Lady," I whisper to myself, "there's another way to look at that." Using those words the lobby manager spoke so long ago became my cue to shift perspectives about him. Either I could understand him to be difficult, or I could understand him to be blessed with an adventurous spirit. The former perspective filled me with worry and the need to control; the latter allowed me to breathe at least somewhat easier and remember that his impulse to explore was just as often as not a true gift.

Sometimes, nowadays, when he sets off, I even feel proud of him.

Susan McCormick

LOVE MAY LOOK FORWARD, AND HATE MAY LOOK BACK,
BUT ANXIETY HAS EYES ALL OVER ITS HEAD.

Mignon McLaughlin

W A Y   8 :

Turn to Others

UNITED WE STAND; DIVIDED WE FALL.

For years, research has indicated that a common human response to difficulty is the "fight-or-flight" phenomenon: that is, acting quickly to either overpower or escape whatever threatens our well-being. Worry—like all other kinds of difficulty—can indeed trigger such responses. As our worry and anxiety about a given situation take hold, we become increasingly compelled to either get on top of it or get away from it. One or the other. Anything—anything at all, please—but sitting there in it, like an overcooked carrot in a stew!

A few years ago while conducting a landmark research study on this issue, Laura Cousin Klein and her colleagues at UCLA noticed something amazing. They observed that those people who do not fall into fight-or-flight behavior often gravitated toward another pattern, which they named "tend-and-befriend." Instead of trying to dominate their environment, they sought to improve it, and instead of trying to overpower or escape other people, they turned to them in a spirit of care and friendship.

The researchers first noticed this tend-and-befriend pattern, oddly enough, by simply noticing their own behavior in the lab. If mistakes or poor choices were made, worry amongst all of them escalated greatly, for there were both funding and time limitations and little room for waste of either. When this happened, some of the scientists would automatically respond in fight-or-flight mode. For instance, they would toss about instruments and papers, aggressively attack one another with verbal criticism, or stomp out of the room in frustration.

Others, however, went a different route, the route of tend-and-befriend. This meant that they began carefully tidying up the lab, sometimes lingering after-hours until its atmosphere was once again orderly and calm. And instead of attacking or blaming one another, they instinctively used solace and encouragement to knit closer bonds with co-workers by chatting, checking in, and inviting one another out for coffee or lunch.

Both modes of response are legitimate. Sometimes, fight-or-flight truly is the wisest choice. In the case of this research lab, however, tend-and-befriend behavior proved far more productive, and served to reduce anxiousness and worry much more effectively. So too in our lives.

If you're worried about the eight-hundred-pound grizzly bear bearing down on you, by all means opt for fight-or-flight! On the other hand, if you're worried about something a little less imminent and less uncompromising, consider tend-and-befriend.

Fight-or-flight is basically an alienating response. It reduces worry by creating some kind of separation from its source, either through domination or absence. It is likely to leave you standing alone.

Tend-and-befriend is basically a relational behavior. It reduces worry by sharing the weight of it with others and creating a nurturing environment that can "hold" the intensity of it in a web of mutuality.

With whom might you share the weight of your worries? Friends and loved ones are a natural first choice. A good friend can sometimes listen without even offering advice, and we will still find the weight of our worries lifted. Often, worry sharing can flow both ways, so that we are supporting one another simultaneously.

At first it may seem that our worries are too silly or small to share, or that no one else would want to hear about them. What I've noticed though, in my own life and the lives of countless others, is that in sharing them I often discover that others worry about the same things. I'm not alone after all! Once that is understood, we and those we care about are in a much better position to help one another.

During his teenage years, one of my sons became notoriously poor about relaying phone messages. This worried me constantly because it had power to impact my professional life—my connections to those who depended upon me as a minister. No matter how many times I begged him to be careful about this, he kept slipping up. I'd be left fielding comments about my own lack of responsiveness to phone requests from congregants.

Finally, one day, a woman from my church called me at around 7 a.m., while he was still fast asleep. "I'm sorry to call you so early," she said, "but I left a message with your son yesterday, and I just knew that if he's anything like my son was as a teenager, he'd probably forget to tell you."

I heaved a silent but sizeable sigh of relief. At last, someone who understood! She took it even further, though. "Don't worry," she added kindly. "He'll outgrow it in a year or two. In the meantime, you might want to try getting some of those marker boards and putting one right by every phone in the house. He can write down messages on the spot then and also doodle to his heart's delight during those long hours he talks to his friends. That worked for us—most of the time anyway!"

My worry dissolved almost immediately. I had encountered not just an understanding heart, but also a solution to my problem. Believe me, I've passed that solution along whenever it has seemed applicable.

Friends and loved ones are not always a good choice for worry help. When they're the source of your worry, for example, that sometimes disqualifies them from being the best listeners. Or if your worries are outside the realm of their experience, they just might not understand. I've seen this happen when people struggle with serious depression, for example. If you are so overwhelmed with worry that you can't sleep at night or can't seem to get yourself off the couch, your friends may not be able to comprehend how truly debilitating your situation is. In such a case, turning to another might mean turning to a psychologist or psychiatrist, a priest, rabbi, or pastor—someone who not only understands, but also has had some professional training in how to help. You will be amazed at the flood of relief you feel as you unburden your worries to another human being that you know you can trust.

For that matter, turning to another doesn't necessarily mean turning to a human being at all! Many of us can testify that whispering worries into the furry, non-judgmental ear of a loyal dog or cat is equivalent to releasing them altogether. Goldfish and parakeets will listen for hours without interruption, and still be there the next morning. They are also excellent at keeping secrets!

In Guatemalan culture, people turn with their worries

to little dolls. These "worry dolls" are usually about one inch tall, created from bits of stick, wire, cloth, and thread. In other words, anyone can make one. According to long-standing tradition, you share your worries with your doll at bedtime, leave it nearby to stand vigil over your dreams, and then reclaim your worries, if need be, in the morning. This allows for a good night's sleep and a peaceful heart.

Prayer is also a way of turning to another, or perhaps I should say Another. The act of prayer can be an act of sharing, unburdening, releasing ourselves into the trust of a loving God, a being with shoulders broad enough, eyes insightful enough, and heart tender enough to carry the weight of even our most overwhelming worries. Some people, uncomfortable for one reason or another with the idea of God, find it easier to release their worries to what they might call angels, guides, or ancestors.

Friends, loved ones, professionals, animals, dolls, prayers, and calls for help to that which we cannot even see are all helpful. Indeed, there remain so many ways in the great length and breadth of the human experience to share worry that I almost wonder if the healing power lies in the act itself more than in any particular method.

Turning to others with our worry can be frightening because it means exposing our vulnerability and running the risk of being misunderstood. But the benefits greatly outweigh the liabilities. As we tend-and-befriend more and more in response to our worries, life almost always becomes easier, lighter, and far more open to the possibility of joy.

AND THEN COMPASSION WILL BE
WEDDED TO POWER
AND SOFTNESS WILL COME TO A WORLD
THAT IS HARSH AND UNKIND . . .
AND THEN EVERYWHERE WILL BE
CALLED EDEN ONCE AGAIN.

Judy Chicago

Turn to Others

- Remember the last five times you got really worried about something. What was your response in each case: "fight-or-flight" or "tend-and-befriend"? Do you have an inclination toward one mode or the other? If you have remembered an incident to which you responded in fight-or-flight mode, re-imagine the ending. How would things have come out if you'd gone instead toward tend and befriend?

- List your true friends: those people who form a circle of support if you need it. Are there people on your list that you have not talked to or maintained contact with that you need to reconnect with? Consider doing so. If there are those on your list that need a thank you or some support from you, reach out to them.

- Make two columns on a single piece of paper. At the top of one, write "Things I Will Worry About Today." At the top of the other, write "Things I Will Let My Guardian Angel Worry About Today." Put a few items in each column and commit to truly turning over what you've chosen not to carry. At the end of the day, look at your lists again. How did you do? For that matter, how did your angel do?

- If you wonder about getting professional help for your worries, check out the WHO Guide to Mental Health in Primary Care (www.whoguidemhpcuk.org) on the Internet. This website reviews several different mental health diagnoses in terms of presenting complaints, diagnostic features, essential information for patients, advice and support resources, and useful medications. It should help you assess the possible need for medical care. A visit with your regular doctor can often also help with this.

- Using materials around the house, make your own worry doll. If your worries feel bigger than what one doll can hold, make several dolls. Make a whole team of them, if you want—with specialist dolls for a particular worry! See what happens tonight when you put them to work and think twice tomorrow morning before you take their burden back. Worry dolls, by the way, make good gifts to friends who have a lot on their minds.

- If prayer is important for you, before you go to bed each night, sit quietly in a chair with your hands on your knees with your palms down. Close your eyes. Take a few slow, deep breaths. Then bring to mind all the worries and fears of the day, all the concerns that will rob you of sleep and raise your blood pressure. Once you have gathered the legion of worries, drop each of them very consciously out of your open palm into the hands of God who will hold on to them overnight (or forever if you wish). When you have let go of each and every worry, turn your hands over, palms up, and ask for the energy or grace that you need to rest and renew yourself.

The soul should always stand ajar. . . .

Emily Dickinson

Brothers

L ouise Wolfgramm is the executive director of AMICUS, a non-profit organization in Minneapolis, Minnesota, that matches prison inmates with volunteers from the outside for the benefit of both. Because prison life itself rarely fosters tend-and-befriend behavior, her AMICUS stories about inmates and volunteers coming together in a spirit of caring are especially poignant.

One story in particular—the story of Ted Jefferson and Cary Humphries—illustrates powerfully how turning to others can diminish worry, fear, and anxiety even under the most unlikely circumstances. The story goes something like this:

Ted Jefferson, from the slums of Milwaukee, had been incarcerated for second-degree murder. He initially looked into AMICUS because he thought being connected to someone from the outside might make the time pass more quickly for him. In a sense he had passed beyond worrying about his life, beyond even being angry, and lived out his days in a state of flat, unending hopelessness. Even so, he filled out the AMICUS forms, writing down information about his background and his interests, so that the staff could come up with some sort of appropriate match for him. They found Cary Humphries.

On the day Cary Humphries was supposed to arrive, Ted sat in the waiting room, which was actually a holding cell with several battered plastic chairs set against the wall, thumbing through old dog-eared magazines. The appointed meeting time came and went, and no one approached him. Ted's only thought was, "Right. This is my life. The guy isn't even gonna show up." The only other person in the room was a man who looked a little like Colonel Sanders, owner of the fried chicken empire: an aristocratic, white haired gentleman with well polished fingernails, an extremely trim beard, and a black leather briefcase. Finally Ted struck up a conversation, more to pass the time than anything else.

"Who you waiting for?"

The man glanced down at a slip of paper in his hand. In a strong southern drawl, he said, "I'm waiting for a man named Ted Jefferson."

Ted's head jerked back in surprise. "I'm Ted Jefferson. You Cary Humphries? I thought for sure you'd be a black guy."

Cary Humphries nodded. "I understand what you mean, Sir. I thought you would be Caucasian. I assumed that AMICUS would take racial considerations into their match."

"Yeah, well, whatever."

The two men stared at one another for a long time.

It was Cary who finally broke the silence. "Well, it's my pleasure to meet you." He smiled and extended his arm for a handshake that Ted Jefferson ignored. "Shall we get to know one another a little?"

Ted's smile was more of a smirk, and inside he was filled with distrust. "Not just a white guy," he was thinking to himself, "but a rich white guy; a rich, southern, white guy. Like I'm supposed to trust him with my troubles?"

The two men attempted conversation for a while. It turned out like it seemed it was going to. They really didn't have anything in common. Ted Jefferson had never held a nine-to-five job. He had always been on the street, a mover and shaker who engaged in erratic and often illegal moneymaking plans. He liked hanging out in bars.

Cary Humphries, on the other hand, had never *not* had a nine-to-five job—actually nine to six, seven, or eight o'clock was more like it. He was a rising star at the Cargill Corporation, a businessman, a southern gent. He had never even been inside a prison before, not once. It was extremely awkward.

"Please, tell me something about yourself."

"Nothing to tell."

Finally, Ted, being a straightforward man by nature, said, "You know, I have to wonder how in the devil they matched us up, you and me. It ain't exactly Starsky and Hutch, is it? You and me, we got nothing the same, nothing to talk about. I'll be doing some praying about that one, that's for sure."

"You pray, do you?" came Cary's curious response.

"Course I pray," answered Ted, irritation in his voice. "How else you think a body survives in a junkyard like this?" Then, catching a strange look in Cary's eye, he snorted with skepticism. "Why do you ask? You pray? You got nothing to pray about, man! Your life, all perfect like that."

"Yes, I do pray," said Cary simply, quietly.

These two men had finally uncovered the sole activity upon which some unknown, now-far-away AMICUS staff member had evidently matched them. And that's what they did that first day. They prayed together.

Ted, reflecting back over the years, would tell others time and time again how it was actually during that first prayer that the constrictions and constraints of his past— the worries, the fears, the deep hopelessness—fell away for just one instant. Getting a brief glimpse at hope for the first time in years, he sensed against all likelihood that Cary would become, somehow, his brother.

Cary, for his part, had the oddest intuition, the strangest feeling, that he had met Ted somewhere before. But he knew that was impossible. There was just something, some barely discernable thing, that fit between the two of them. He could sense it in his bones.

Cary and Ted met regularly through the duration of Ted's prison term, praying together and very gradually coming to know and trust one another. Each time they met, Ted's secret worries about not being good enough, capable enough, smart enough, to survive on the outside dissolved just the slightest little bit. And Cary's secret worries about being too self-centered, too greedy, too arrogant to really help another human being in need dissolved just the slightest little bit as well.

Whether they liked it or not, they needed one another deeply in order to recover from their respective self-doubts.

It would have been much easier for them to isolate from one another, dislike or even hate one another, to choose, without thinking, the old familiar fight-or-flight response. But they were both brave enough to do otherwise.

And that's why, by the time Ted was released from prison, their respective skills and dreams had come together to form a single powerful vision. Ted Jefferson and Cary Humphries went into business together. They opened a halfway house, a way station for newly released inmates, a place where people could receive help and support in finding their way back to normal life on the outside.

Cary, ever the businessman, took charge of the funding. Using his connections and his financial expertise, he brought to their endeavor a solid underpinning of support from the broader community. Ted, ever the go-getter, knew how to run that house. He understood exactly what the residents were going through, exactly what they needed, and exactly how to get it for them. They were the perfect team.

If these two men hadn't turned to one another when the opportunity presented itself, something very important would have never come into being. If they hadn't found some way to bring their whole selves to one another— fears, worries, gifts, failures, successes, the whole package—something very important would have been lost. True to his instinct on the very first day they met, Ted called Cary his brother until the day he died.

WE ARE CAUGHT IN AN INESCAPABLE NETWORK OF MUTUALITY, TIED IN A SINGLE GARMENT OF DESTINY.

Martin Luther King, Jr.

Something

Igrew up in a house where there was lots of fighting and lots of violence. My father never hurt us four kids, but if he began drinking at dinnertime, which happened pretty often, there was no telling what he might do to my mother after we went to bed. I remember lying in that bed scared to death, just listening to the terrible sounds coming up the stairs: shouts, curses, accusations, crashing furniture. I feel kind of sick still, just remembering.

I was the youngest of the four of us, by a long shot actually. Sometimes, when I was so worried about my mom that I couldn't stand it any more, I'd tiptoe out of my room and lean over the upstairs banister, listening even though I hated what I heard and wondering what would happen to me if I went down there to help her. Often, I'd find my big brothers and sister already out there, leaning over the banister themselves. The four of us would huddle together in the cold night air, barefoot and shivering, each one of us comforted by the understanding that we were, at least, not alone in our terror.

In a funny kind of way, the fighting brought us kids together more than we probably would have been otherwise. None of my friends seemed to have homes like this, and I would never have thought to try to tell them. I was way too ashamed. My big sister and brothers though, they understood. Without any words at all, they understood. We all helped each other.

I probably don't have to tell you that this was the kind of house that kids leave as soon as they can figure out a way. By the time I was eight, my sister had found a job and moved to a different state. By the time I was ten, both my brothers had left for college. That left me alone. Alone with the fear, the worry, and the despair. I was so scared.

My brothers and my sister tried to comfort and reassure me before they left, telling me I'd be all right and things like that. In retrospect, I bet they felt guilty leaving me, but just couldn't stand staying, for their own sake. I had to figure out how to make it on my own.

I don't know if this is common or not, but over the years, things didn't get better. They got worse. I guess if you consider that alcoholism is a progressive disease, it makes sense that my dad gradually began drinking every night. My mom, probably to cope with it at first but then for her own reasons, began drinking right along with him. So every night was a nightmare.

My grades in school were pretty crummy, and I was distracted all the time. No teacher thought to ask me what was going on at home. It was my big, ugly secret. And even if they had asked, I'm not so sure I would have had the guts to tell them.

One night, the fighting seemed especially bad. I had learned to not go out in the hall any more. It was too cold and lonely without my sister and brothers. So I just lay there listening. That night I felt more alone than I ever had, more scared, more sad, more worried, more powerless, and more hopeless than I ever had. This was more than I could bear. At that exact moment, the very moment I felt overwhelmed beyond hope, I suddenly had the strangest feeling. It was the feeling of something or someone infinitely tender, infinitely loving and caring, holding me, holding me in arms so strong that nothing on earth could ever make them let me go.

You'd think this would have scared me just because it was real, but also so strange and different. Actually, it didn't scare me at all. In fact, this thing—whatever it was— seemed to absorb the terror right out of me. Gradually I relaxed, and felt secure, and strangest of all knew that, somehow or another, I was going to be all right. No matter what happened, I was going to be all right. I wasn't alone after all, no matter how lonely it felt.

The sounds of the fighting downstairs continued, but I rested deeply into this gentle warmth, this gentle tenderness, that had mysteriously come to help me. It was the greatest blessing I have ever received in my life, almost as though some great force had been watching over me all along, saw that I had reached a point of no return, and come to help me.

I never had that same experience again after that night, but I never forgot it either. What was it? Was it God? Was it some kind of angel? Was it a figment of my imagination? Some kind of psychotic break with reality?

I've thought about that a lot, over the years, and come to the conclusion that it doesn't really matter. What I learned on that terrifying night so long ago was that I am not alone. No matter what. There are people—like my brothers and sister—who can sometimes help me carry my burden by understanding and being there, and then, when the people can't help any more, there is, I've come to believe, Something Else. Something that is there for me even when all of humanity fails. Something about love and care and tenderness beyond compare. Something I can trust. Even if I can't prove it.

That kind of childhood hardly gave me a good solid start in life. I mean, I had a lot to learn that never was shown to me as a child, and a lot of my lessons involved big mistakes, big bumps, tumbles, and bruises. But through it all, I've known about that Something, and gained tremendous strength from it.

I take no step, I meet no challenge, I bear no burden, alone.

John

I WILL FEAR NO EVIL,

FOR YOU ARE WITH ME;

YOUR ROD AND STAFF, THEY COMFORT ME.

Psalm 23

WAY 9 :

Live in the Present

PAST AND FUTURE VEIL GOD FROM OUR
SIGHT;
BURN UP BOTH OF THEM WITH FIRE.

Rumi

Ours is not a culture conducive to living in the present, free from preoccupation with the past or future. In fact, we operate a multi-million dollar industry—the insurance industry—based upon our impulse to worry about what might happen in the future and our parallel need to protect ourselves from undesirable outcomes as thoroughly as possible.

If we were able to tape record our thoughts for even one day, we would probably listen back only to learn that the majority of our mental time is spent in the past: Why did I do it that way? What did he or she think of me? How did we end up going in that direction? Or the future: How will I ever find time for that? By when do I need to finish this? What if I can't get to the next thing on time? Proportionately, for most of us, little time is spent dwelling in the present.

The quadrant diagram in chapter 1 of this book illustrates how worry tends to emerge in situations over which we feel little control. If that is the case, then both the past and the future are fertile ground for it: the past being eternally out of reach behind us and the future moving as it does forever before us like a mirage in the desert. To accept both past and future as beyond our control and move into the present moment wholeheartedly is to set oneself free from worry in significant ways.

Often people will agree with me about the past being beyond our control, but they will hesitate or even disagree with me about the future. They might say by way of example that to ignore preparing for future retirement or sending kids to college is not only risky, but even foolish. Yes, I agree. But planning for the future is one thing, and worrying about it quite another. When we plan for something, we make choices that will serve our needs in years ahead and then return to the present in a better frame of mind, more confident, relaxed, and free to enjoy life.

When we worry about something in the future, however, we allow it to fill our thoughts and drain our energies in ways that actually prevent us from being confident or relaxed in the present moment. When this happens, neither the present nor the future is well served. But what does it even look like to live in the present moment?

Think of a time when you were so engaged, so caught up, in what you were doing that you literally lost track of the time. Perhaps you were out working in your garden on a beautiful day and surprised to notice that the sun was "suddenly" beginning to set. Or maybe you took your watch off to play a game of tennis and were having so much fun that you never once glanced down at your wrist by mistake to see if your court time was up. Perhaps you got caught up in a great book on a rainy day and just let yourself read all the way through to the end, lost in the story. When we truly allow ourselves to live in the present moment, we become in some sense joyous, whole, and at peace. Worry can only dissolve.

One might think that if the present moment is a difficult one—containing pain or sorrow—then worry might spring up even there as well. Interestingly though, research is beginning to indicate that much of our pain or worry about the present has to do with how we interpret our past and what we project into our future. For example, people with intense pain might find the present moment difficult and worrisome. But if they "watch themselves" for a while, they are likely to notice that they are carrying not just the present pain itself, but also painful memories of how their condition came to be and painful fears about a future in which they can never get free of it. In other words, their suffering is multiplied by three.

Often, learning to focus thought on the present moment alone can significantly reduce their pain—and their worry about their pain—after all kinds of other treatments and medications have failed.

Living in the present moment, concentrating on what is versus what has been or will be, is one of those arts that is simple but not easy. It goes, for most of us, against habit. There are all kinds of books written about it. Many meditative practices have been developed to increase our capacity for it. Great athletes or other heroes and heroines often model it for us. One interesting exercise for staying in the present, initially developed by Dr. Carolyn Myss, from her video "Why People Don't Heal and How They Can," goes something like this:

Imagine that every morning when you arise the universe allots you a certain amount of energy; let's describe it in financial terms and call it $100. By energy, I mean energy to create, energy to love, energy to make your own life and the broader world a better place—physically, emotionally, mentally, and spiritually. So you have this $100 to spend as you see fit. If you underspend and have some left over at the end of the day, you can save it to some extent, but not in large quantities. A person cannot, for example, expend little energy for a thousand days and then move a mountain on the thousand-and-first. Basically, in this scenario, savings accounts are irrelevant. It makes more sense to spend what you've got each day as best you can and let go of the rest.

If you overspend, on the other hand, using up more than your allotted $100 in a given day, your body can float you a small loan by squeezing energy out of its own resources and strength. But overspending day after day gets dangerous, for it will eventually deplete you, leaving you sick, weak, and tired.

The art of this exercise, then, is to gratefully receive your daily $100 for the mysterious gift that it is, and then spend it as best you can in twenty-four hours, according to your own values and intentions. Each new day, you begin again.

One of Myss's concerns is that we seem to be a nation of "overspenders." We try to do too much, we worry too much, we set unreasonably high standards for ourselves, and we exhaust or deplete our energies far too consistently. This, she says, is at least one of the reasons why we have so many health problems, despite the relative excellence of our nation's medical care. She adds that we also tend to be unconscious spenders. We leap out of bed and go through our days at such a frantic pace that we don't even notice where we're spending our dollars. Like game show contestants with just one fast chance to spend, spend, spend before the buzzer goes off, we toss our bills here and there all willy-nilly, seeking desperately to purchase we-know-not-what. If we were to slow down and notice, we would be shocked to learn how much energy we spend—well, waste—on worries, regrets, unresolved sorrows, unrealistic expectations, and projected fears. How much we waste, in other words, on the past and the future.

Myss's funding exercise invites us to become intentional about budgeting for the present day, and the present day only. I remember the first time I tried it out as the mother of a teenage son with diabetes. From dawn to dusk I watched myself carefully, trying to get a bead on how and where I was investing my energy—my thoughts, actions, and desires. The first thing I did when my son came down for breakfast and chose food less than ideal for a diabetic was to automatically drop a wad of energy-cash on worry about his future, projecting out to a day where the complications of the illness would make his life miserable. This preoccupied me until after he had left for school.

Now I could have spent that same energy in a "Walk for Diabetes" marathon or learning about some tempting new recipes. But I hadn't exactly learned to budget yet. Later that day at work, I was asked to make a chaplaincy visit with a young cystic fibrosis patient. At that point, I accidentally spent a big chunk of energy-change on worry about the past, wondering how it was that kids got chronic illnesses like this. Then I asked myself for the umpteenth time what I might have done to cause my son's diabetes or what I should have done to prevent it. I could have spent that same energy on making this child laugh and bringing a little extra boost of joy to her day. But my sense of regret was just too pricey, and it consumed more of my available resources than I meant it to. And so on and so forth.

You get the idea. In a way, Myss's funding exercise isn't all that imaginary. We wake from sleep each morning with just one day in front of us and just one allotment of energy with which to shape it. We are free to spend it in so many ways. It's all a matter of what we choose.

WORRYING IS WASTING TODAY'S TIME CLUTTERING UP TOMORROW'S OPPORTUNITIES WITH YESTERDAY'S TROUBLES.

Anonymous

Live in the Present

- Try the funding exercise for yourself. This is best accomplished if you keep track of things in writing. You can even begin with a checkbook ledger, $100 written in as the starting balance. Pay attention to the "checks" you write all day. Record them carefully. This will take some guesswork and intuition. Then "balance" your ledger in the evening before bedtime. Did you spend your energy in the ways you meant to? Did you overspend or underspend? What did you learn about yourself? What would you like to do differently tomorrow?

- Investor Burton Castle's strategy uses the concept of the "stop-loss order." This term refers to a practice in the investment world. If a stock is presently valued at $50 per share, for example, Castle will instruct that it be automatically sold if it drops to $45, whether that happens in a day, a week, or three years out. He knows then that he has blocked his losses and can cease to worry about the future.

- So how might this look in your life? Let's say your friend is always late, sometimes quite late. You, on the other hand, always arrive punctually then sit there worrying about how much time you'll have to waste waiting for him. Put a stop-loss order on this situation. Decide that you will wait (and worry) for only twenty minutes, no more, before leaving to do something else. In all fairness, tell your friend about this plan!

- This exercise honors the now and affirms our presence in this moment without the worries of the past or concerns for the future. It can be done for as long as you wish, anywhere, anytime, in any position. Focusing on our breathing calms us, slows our heart rate, and yet is energizing. By consciously choosing to smile, we affirm the goodness of the present moment. Smiling relaxes us. Since the purpose of the exercise is to pay attention to and affirm the present moment, you might keep your eyes open. Breathe slowly, deeply, and evenly.

  - During one or two breaths say:
  - "Breathing in, I calm my body."
  - "Breathing out, I smile."
  - After one or two breaths, continue for about fifteen breaths:

- Breathing in say, "Calm."
- Breathing out say, "Smile."
- Continue until you feel calm, relaxed, and ready for phase two:
- During one or two breaths say:
- "Breathing in, I live in the present moment."
- "Breathing out, I know it is a wonderful moment."
- After one or two breaths, continue for as long as you like:
- Breathing in say, "Present moment."
- Breathing out say, "Wonderful moment."

(This exercise is adapted from *The Blooming of the Lotus* by Thich Nhat Hanh.)

- You can practice being present where you are while you do any task. For instance, when you are doing housework, just do one thing at a time. As you scrub the toilet, just scrub the toilet. As you vacuum the living room carpet, concentrate on vacuuming. If you become distracted just remind yourself gently, "I'm vacuuming now." Thus, housework becomes a kind of meditation. Besides, you work more efficiently when you do one thing at a time.

YOU CAN'T START WORRYING ABOUT WHAT'S GOING TO HAPPEN.

YOU GET SPASTIC ENOUGH WORRYING ABOUT WHAT'S HAPPENING NOW.

Lauren Bacall

A Dazzling Moment

C hildren have a lot to teach us sometimes.

Being the receptionist in a small town doctor's office means offering hospitality to all ages. Lots of times, parents have no choice but to bring their kids along, and the little ones end up with me in the waiting room while their mother or father goes back to see the doctor.

I like kids a lot! That's why our office has a little table with chairs and a box of toys. But the thing the kids love most is the bowl that sits on my desk. It's a big bowl, and I keep it filled with miscellaneous treats—Band-Aids with cartoon characters on them, tiny pads of paper and pencils, pretty shells and rocks and trinkets, pretend eyeglasses, little puzzles, those kinds of things. All the children who come into our office are welcome to rummage around and find something for themselves in there.

Just last week, the strangest thing happened. It had been a bad day. Life wasn't going so well for me at home, and I had been worrying about a fight I'd had the night before with my husband. Furthermore—and isn't this how it always goes—the office had been so busy I felt completely exhausted. Here it was dusk already, and my desk was strewn with unfinished reports, appointments scrawled on Post-it notes that needed to be entered into the computer, files that needed to be put away—just a bunch of junk.

Just as I was sitting there in my slump, in walked a little girl, a strikingly beautiful child with jet black hair and smiling eyes. She didn't seem unhappy or lost, but she also didn't seem to have any parent with her. She looked to be about five years old. "Is your mom or dad around?" I asked, hoping this wasn't going to be too complicated.

"At the dentist," she said. That meant she had wandered over from the waiting room of the dentist's office across the hall. I didn't mind. It happened pretty often. We visited for a moment and, even though she was willing to talk to me, I could tell that her eyes were glued to my bowl. I invited her to help herself.

Once given permission to explore this bowl, she was not really interested in me anymore and didn't pretend otherwise. That was fine with me. It gave me an opportunity to watch her unnoticed as she rummaged around.

First she found—and stared at for a very long time—a plastic dime store ring with a very large, sparkly, gaudy pink glass jewel in it. She slipped it on her finger, her eyes bright with joy. I was about to say something like, "Thanks for coming," or "Glad you like it," when I noticed that her gaze had already returned, with yearning, to my bowl. She wanted to keep going.

Normally, I would stop a child from taking too much, but something about the look on her face held me back. "What the heck," I thought to myself. "Everybody needs two prizes instead of just one, some days." She reached in and picked out another dime store ring, similar to the first, this time with three smaller purple glass stones in a row. She slipped that one on her hand. I looked at how caught up she was, how happy she was, and just decided to keep quiet.

By the time this little girl had put the fifth ring on, her hand looked absolutely dazzling, a virtual rainbow of faceted colors. There were a million unspoken comments running through my head—comments about sharing, about being greedy, about asking permission. At the same time, though, there was just something about her. Watching her more carefully, through the eyes of tenderness, I could see that she was not really a selfish or greedy child at all. She was, rather, simply drawn to that which sparkled, that which seemed beautiful to her. And she was wisely allowing herself to enjoy it.

Unlike me, she was not worried about things at home, about past failures or future fears. She was not stressed out by what she had lost or could not attain. It was much simpler than that. She was just focusing all of her attention on the present moment, a moment that dazzled with beauty for her. Plain as that. If I told her to stop, she'd stop, no doubt. But she would not stop herself. Why interrupt something this much fun for no reason?

I was really beginning to enjoy this! I watched in respectful silence as she selected and put on rings number six, seven, eight, and nine from the bowl. Just as I was wondering what ring number ten would look like, she mysteriously came to a halt. Looking straight at me with a wordless but deeply joyous smile of gratitude, she turned on her heel then and walked out.

That night, on the way home from the office, I just decided on a whim to stop at the store. I carefully selected a cut of good beef—my husband's favorite—and some fresh broccoli. Into the cart went some crusty French bread, a double chocolate cake, a bouquet of flowers. When I got to the ice cream and knew I didn't need it, I suddenly understood about the tenth ring. Sometimes, the sheer pleasure of the moment fills you, and is sufficient. I set out for home.

Nancy Mason

A CRUST EATEN IN JOY IS BETTER THAN
A BANQUET PARTAKEN IN ANXIETY.

Aesop

The Day He Didn't Propose

Though I am growing old and have been married to my
dear wife, Mae, for over forty years, we will probably
both always remember what I've come to call "The Day He
Didn't Propose."

We had been going together for several months and
grown quite fond of one another. My mother made it clear,
in her own subtle way, that she considered Mae to be the
one I should spend my life with. It was true that we were
quite compatible. We loved going dancing together and
skating on the lake in winter. We both attended the
Methodist church in town, and both wanted to have
children one day. Mae was just finishing up at the
university, trained to be a schoolteacher. I had already
completed my degree in engineering and held down a
good job that would provide for us quite well. Clearly, the
stage was set for us getting more serious, but I was at heart
a young man yet, wild and foolish in my ways, and I just
wasn't paying much attention I guess.

When Mae's twenty-first birthday got close, I knew I wanted to get her something special, something that would surprise her, maybe sweep her off her feet a little. I thought about it long and hard, and finally decided that I would give her a ride in a hot air balloon. It was expensive, granted, but it'd be like a dream come true, I thought, to be sailing with my sweetheart up in the sky like that, blue sky all around us, all the people below as tiny as toys. Maybe we could even sneak a smooch or two up there. I found a man that offered balloon rides about twenty miles away and set the big date. This was going to be great!

When I picked Mae up on the day of her birthday, she looked especially pretty and had on a new dress. I still hadn't told her what her present was, and she was just glowing with anticipation of my surprise. We drove together out past the edge of the city. It was a beautiful day, clear and warm, with just the slightest breeze. I could hardly wait to see the look on her face when she realized the treat she was in for.

Mae and I chatted and laughed all along the way, until we pulled onto the gravel road that led to our destination. There stood a big sign, red painted letters with a blue and green painted balloon alongside them, reading "Lenny's Hot Air Balloon Rides, This Way!"

Mae's face went pale. "I didn't expect us to come here," she said in a funny voice. "Is this the gift?"

At first I didn't notice that anything had changed. "Yup, this is it!" I blurted out in naive excitement. "Happy birthday, Darling! From me to you, this is it!"

Mae tried to smile. To her credit, she tried real hard. But as we bumped along down the dusty gravel road, I glanced over and could see that she had begun silently crying. She had a handkerchief over her eyes, and her shoulders were shaking. And even I could tell she wasn't laughing. I pulled over to the side of the road, confounded in a way that only foolish young men can be. "What's wrong, Mae? What's wrong, Darling?" I gingerly put my arm around her.

She tried to deny that anything was wrong at all, but nobody on earth would have bought that one. Finally she blurted it out. "I had thought—I had thought you got me an engagement ring for my birthday. I had thought you were taking me to some quiet, romantic place, so you could get down on your knees and ask me to marry you."

I felt so ashamed of myself. I felt so stupid. Here was Mae, in love and wanting to tie the knot forever, and here was I, dreaming up cockamamie schemes about floating through the clouds, without even thinking things through from her angle. But aside from feeling ashamed and stupid, I also felt kind of scared. I mean, this young woman was dead serious about me. We were in quite a pickle.

What she did next made me love her all the more. She dried her eyes, tucked her hanky up her sleeve in that way she does even to this day, turned to me, and said, "Well, even though it did catch me off guard, I think I could really enjoy a hot air balloon ride on a pretty day like this. Let's not worry about that other for now. Let's go take our turn and enjoy ourselves. How about it?"

That's what she taught me, and that's what she teaches me still, my Mae. Life is full of ups and downs, expectations and disappointments. You can worry about what went wrong, or take what you've got and be glad about it. You can fret about what might not come through, or take what you've got and be glad about it.

It was beautiful that day, up in the clouds. And she was beautiful. Not once did she bring up what had happened.

She was too busy taking in the sky, holding my hand, and appreciating the gift I had given her—just as it was.

As soon as I could save up enough, I bought her a ring, got down on my knees, and asked her to marry me. And I have never once—for all these forty years—regretted it.

James Tyler

LOVE THE MOMENT, AND THE ENERGY OF THE MOMENT WILL SPREAD BEYOND ALL BOUNDARIES.

Corita Kent

WAY 10:

Entrust Yourself to Joy

WHEN NOTHING IS SURE, EVERYTHING
IS POSSIBLE.

Margaret Drabble

Worry—if we let it—can greatly diminish joy. In a way, worry and joy are opposites. Incompatibles. Worry pulls our thoughts into the past, and all that has gone wrong, then tosses them toward the future and all that might go wrong next. Joy, on the other hand, draws our thoughts fully into the present moment, and all that is right about it, all that is beautiful and delightful and worthy of celebration.

Worry, in one sense, is the safer path, for it leaves us nothing to lose. After all, if the past has seemed grim and the future looks to be grim still, well, the present becomes not only fairly unimportant, but also quite predictable. A dependable kind of thing, a thing that requires little of us in the way of trust or courage.

That's why choosing joy often involves at least some degree of willingness to risk. You might protest the word "choose" here. Worry rarely feels like a choice in the first place. It seems more like something that comes over us, quite uninvited, despite our best efforts to ward it off. But in the end, worry—and joy too, for that matter—may well be more of a choice than we would initially suspect.

Consider the ancient Buddhist tale of the man out on a limb. This is clearly a man who has everything to worry about. Walking along innocently, minding his own business, he has accidentally stepped off the edge of a steep cliff. Desperately, he has grabbed one thin branch at the cliff's rim and dangles now over the edge of the deadly precipice.

First he tries to scramble back up onto safe ground, but there is no place to get a footing, and the branch—thin and wobbly at best—seems about to be uprooted from the sandy cliff-side loam in which it grows. Next he looks down, and sees that the bottom of the cliff, a rock bed, is hundreds and hundreds of feet below. Furthermore, three hungry tigers are pacing back and forth there on the rocks, waiting for him to fall, for they want to tear him to pieces.

He can't go up, and he can't go down. He's trapped in a terrible place. His mind races here and there, in search of escape, tormented. Just then he happens to notice that a small, straggly strawberry bush is growing near him, off the side of the cliff. Though it looks sickly, there is one little strawberry growing on it, ripe now, and red as a jewel. What should he do? What should he choose?

He chooses to hold on to the branch with one hand, so that he can pluck the strawberry with the other. He puts the tender little fruit into his mouth. He can barely believe how breathtakingly delicious it is. The man has chosen to entrust himself to joy.

This does not mean that he will not fall to the tigers and rocks soon. In fact, he will, and he knows it. All it means is that, given the choice between paying attention to the strawberry or paying attention to disaster, he chooses the strawberry. In Buddhist tradition, this is a teaching tale. It models the human capacity—quite difficult to achieve, yet worthy of anyone's aspiration—to celebrate wholeheartedly the joy of the moment instead of keeping our focus on suffering.

For me, the most wonderful part of being a hospice chaplain is witnessing the miraculous way this story plays out in the lives of my patients. Their terminal diagnosis—the very painful news that they will die soon—is their own version of a stumble off a cliff. They didn't necessarily see it coming, and they didn't necessarily do a single thing to cause it. Yet, it has happened to them, and they must deal with the tragedy of it. The fragile limb they cling to now is their own clinging to life itself. They know how insufficient the limb is, how it might snap at any minute. Even so, having lost all solid footing, they come to understand the present time as the only thing they have left to hold on to.

They have already tried to climb up on solid ground again, using all the gifts of modern medicine and science, but to no avail. And they have looked down below as well, and have seen the pacing, prowling presence of certain death. So here they dangle. What will they do? How will they handle their lives now?

Granted, dying and moving toward joy are processes and do not happen overnight. But almost always, given any chance to ponder it at all, I see my patients choose to invest their brief remaining time in the preciousness of the simple joys that surround them. A visit from a loved one, the mounting and decorating of a Christmas tree, a favorite song, a prayer, a touch, a kiss, a photograph, a view out a window, a memory shared, an apology offered at last—any or all of these become as miraculously delicious as the strawberry in the story. In other words, my patients choose to entrust themselves not to the tigers and rocks below or the cliff rim above or the fragile limb to which they cling. Bravely, simply, they choose to entrust themselves to joy.

Let's face it: you and I will one day be exactly where they are now. If they can learn how to lean into joy, perhaps we can too.

THE LITTLE CARES THAT FRETTED ME.

I LOST THEM YESTERDAY

AMONG THE FIELDS ABOVE THE SEA.

Elizabeth Barrett Browning

Entrust Yourself to Joy

- Pick a situation that you worry about often and ponder how it parallels the Buddhist tale. What are the cliffs, the limb, the rocks, and the tigers in your situation? What might be the strawberry? How might you reach out and pick it to eat?

- Reflect back upon your childhood (the earlier the better) and recall one thing—an event, a day, a place, a friend— that you loved deeply and that allowed you to abandon yourself to sheer, pure happiness. Reflect upon it until it becomes real in your imagination. Pick three words to describe it. Now scan your present life for something those same three words could describe. If it isn't there, ask yourself how to go about finding it.

- Get up tomorrow morning or go to bed tonight doing one thing differently: one thing more delightful, more fun, more life-giving, and filled with joy. Resolve to let these times of day to be your reminders, for they parallel life's greater edges of birth and death.

- Each night before bed, recall three blessings of the day. You might offer your list to a loved one. Or write them down—every night. This simple spiritual discipline plants seeds of joyous memory and becomes a habit of leaning into joy.

DON'T WORRY THAT YOUR LIFE WILL END; WORRY THAT IT WILL NEVER BEGIN.

Anonymous

A Simple-But-Not-Easy Pleasure

My yoga teacher, a wonderful woman in her early fifties, is kind and gentle. I have never seen her correct a student. Instead she simply shows us a pose and holds it until we have all conformed to it as best we can.

Granted, we are not high-powered or particularly intense yogis. We're middle-aged folks, mostly women, who come one day a week to the local church after long, stressful days to stretch, be still, visit with one another, and remember how good it feels to care for our bodily health. We don't need, and in fact would probably resist, a teacher who demanded precision or even intense dedication.

Sometimes as we move from downward dog to child's pose to mountain pose and so forth, our teacher will talk to us and tell us stories. I've never asked her why. I think this may be her unique way of helping us forget that we are doing something hard or challenging. Caught up in the story, we forget to be anxious about our own performance or ability to bend this way and that.

One day in early January, she began to tell us stories about her New Year's resolutions over the years. Always, she informed us, her resolutions had been focused on what she was worried about, what she feared failing, or ways she felt inadequate. As we stretched from one pose to the next, she went on to illustrate. In her twenties, she said, her resolutions were mostly about trying to be fit and strong: she promised herself she would run every day, or lift weights, or swim. In her thirties—the childbearing years—these resolutions gave way to a decade or so of resolutions about either getting the house organized, or getting out of the house altogether. She'd commit to cleaning out the basement that year or going to the movies every Saturday night. In her forties, the resolutions shifted again in nature, this time to commitments about parenting teens or building her business.

Through all these years and all these resolutions, she told us, one theme was continually present: she would eventually just give up. She'd begin in January full of good intentions, and then—invariably—just fizzle out. Quit. We could all relate to that part of the story and wondered what she would tell us next.

When New Year's Day of her fiftieth year came around she was determined to pick a resolution that would stick. It wasn't as if she had nothing to worry about, nothing to improve upon or change in her life. She often felt slower, heavier, stiffer in the limbs, and less energetic than she had in the past. Her children had grown to young adults, and there was the whole empty nest thing to figure out. Her husband had developed health problems. Life was far from perfect; it held plenty of room for improvement.

Even so, she remembered this time how it had felt to fail at her own resolutions year after year, the quiet disappointment, the elevated sense of failure, one more small but precious piece of self-confidence chipped away every January. Having grown wiser and more thoughtful, she pondered her choice carefully this time and was intentional about shaping it in such a way that she could not, would not, fail.

"And I didn't fail!" she said at last with glee in her voice at the very memory. "That was the first year I kept my resolution all year long!"

Had we been in the most contorted of yoga poses at that moment, we would have been able to hold our positions for a good long time. We were perfectly quiet, entirely captivated. After all, this was January, and we all held precarious resolutions in our own hearts. Finally one of us asked. "So what was your resolution that year?"

"That was the year I resolved to eat one candy bar every single day for the entire year," she said quietly. Our own laughter broke the silence that had settled in the room. We let go of our poses to gasp, giggle, and hear a little more.

"It wasn't easy, but I did it," she told us. "Some nights, I had to even get in the car just before midnight and drive to a twenty-four-hour gas station, just to pick up my daily candy bar. Those were the toughest times, but mostly, it was just a matter of gentle discipline. And let me tell you, it felt great. Finally, I had figured out how to avoid setting myself up. That was my finest year—the year of the great resolution."

To me, eating a candy bar a day sounded like so much indulgence that I would never have allowed myself to even consider it. It was a preposterous resolution—filled with humor and delight—and chocolate. She had simply ditched her worries about weight and correctness, past and future, and gone for the gusto. I loved it. She had entrusted herself to joy. Not in some complex way that involved growth or goodness or political correctness or self-improvement. Just simply. Simply chosen pleasure. And for a whole year.

I had to ask. "So what was your resolution the year after that?" I wanted to know. "That would be a hard one to top."

She smiled at me in her gentle way. "After that year," she said, "I quit making New Year's resolutions altogether."

LIFE IS NOT MEASURED BY THE NUMBER
OF BREATHS WE TAKE,
BUT BY THE MOMENTS THAT TAKE OUR
BREATH AWAY.

Dick Johnson

Presents for Everyone

Our hospice team works hard together to help people die with dignity and with plenty of access to comfort and tenderness. Sometimes our work seems most difficult during a certain stage in the dying process, close to the end of life when a person becomes anxious and agitated. At that point, a person will often want to get up out of bed, even though they are far too weak to do so. Sometimes they will tell family members that they need keys to their car or a ride somewhere. They're apt to express frustration or even anger when loved ones tell them that these things are simply not possible.

Needless to say, their urgency and insistence can be difficult for family members to bear. Those who love them, who would do almost anything at that point to help them, find it quite painful to turn down their requests. And yet, to do otherwise could cause serious harm and suffering. And as if that were not hard enough, this stage often requires much more attentive care. Patients at this point, usually semi-confused but determined to get up, are prone to stumbling, falling out of bed, or hurting themselves in any number of other ways. They require greatly increased vigilance.

It was this stage that Jack O'Malley had entered when his family called upon our team for emergency help. He had fallen twice already by trying to go to the bathroom by himself, despite their pleas to let them help. They'd been forced to lock the doors to their home from the inside and hide the keys because he was trying to get up repeatedly in the night and find his way out the door. It was midwinter in Minnesota, and his wife was fearful that he'd somehow manage to find a way out and then freeze in the snow.

We did what we could: adjusted his medication, assured him that both physically and spiritually this was a time for him to rest, to be at peace. We also spent time supporting his anxious, loving family, trying to normalize this stage for them and emphasize what a wonderful job they were doing in a tough situation.

Most often, when Jack came out of confusion enough to speak, he told us he wanted to go to K-Mart. He was not willing—perhaps not able—to tell us why. We assumed that this desire and this destination were simply manifestations of his disoriented, agitated state of mind. For three days he struggled, sometimes staying up all night, to get to K-Mart. His family took turns watching him vigilantly, trying to soothe him and help him think about other things.

At last, on the morning of the fourth day, Jack relaxed. When our team arrived that morning, his family was gathered about him, exhausted but calm. Jack himself was a changed man. Closer to death now but deeply at peace, he lay on a hospital bed in the living room, eyes closed, beatific expression on his countenance. His arms were resting on the blanket that his wife had tucked lovingly about him. He seemed to be moving in and out of consciousness, no longer speaking more than a few words at a time.

We whispered back and forth about how he was doing, not wanting to disturb him. At one point I said quietly to the others, "Well, I suppose we'll never know why our friend wanted to get to K-Mart so much." Jack, eyes still closed, mumbled something that nobody could quite understand.

"What did you say, Dear?" his wife asked, leaning closer to him.

Jack said it again, this time more clearly. "K-Mart. Presents for all of you. I wanted to get presents. For everyone." And then he lapsed again into unconsciousness.

Even disoriented and confused, Jack had actually been trying to expend his last hours, his final surge of energy, bringing the joy of a gift to others. His wife's eyes filled with tears, and she took his hand. "Well you know it's the thought that counts," she said to him. "Thank you, Dear, for that thought. And we promise that some day soon, we'll all go to K-Mart and pick something nice out for ourselves. And it'll be on you. Presents for everyone, just like you said." He smiled just slightly.

I took a lesson from that moment. A dying man in the midst of profound agitation and discomfort and about to depart from the world itself, about to bid good-bye to everything and everyone he loved, had dedicated his final energies to bringing about happiness. He had wanted his life to culminate in service to generosity and joy. Did he know, somehow, with the mysterious wisdom that can only come to us at the end, that joy really is the most important thing? I like to think he did.

When I become stressed, when I grow anxious about how something will come out, when I let life's problems become the most important thing in a given day, I think of Jack and remind myself that they are probably not. The most important thing may not be our trouble, our worry, our sorrow and tumult, or anything at all along those lines. It may be—really and truly—presents for everyone.

Sometimes I wonder. What would have happened if during the racial trouble in Chicago and Selma, during the tortured times of Vietnam and Desert Storm, during the riots in Los Angeles or the explosions of hatred and cruelty in New York, someone had simply stopped everything, gone to K-Mart, and picked up presents for everyone?

Nancy Waldman

IN THE END, ONLY KINDNESS MATTERS.

Anonymous

Gretchen Thompson is presently a chaplain through Allina Health Systems, and a writer-in-residence at United Theological Seminary of the Twin Cities. She is an ordained Unitarian Universalist minister who has served First Universalist Church in Minneapolis, Unity Church—Unitarian in St. Paul, and the Unitarian Church of Willmar, Minnesota. Her other professional experience has included teaching English and working in hospice and mental health chaplaincy. She holds a Bachelor of Arts from Carleton College and a Masters of Divinity from United Theological Seminary. Her previous books include *Slow Miracles* (1995), *Souls Magnified* (1998) and *God Knows Caregiving Can Pull You Apart* (Sorin Books, 2002). She lives in Minneapolis.